Success in GCSE

for AQA/A

Folens

Alex Josephy
Suzanne Burley
Consultant: John Nield

© 2002 Folens Limited, on behalf of the authors.

United Kingdom: Folens Publishers, Apex Business Centre, Boscombe Road, Dunstable, LU5 4RL.
Email: folens@folens.com

Ireland: Folens Publishers, Greenhills Road, Tallaght, Dublin 24.
Email: info@folens.ie

Poland: JUKA, ul. Renesansowa 38, Warsaw 01-905.

Editor: Kay Macmullan
Layout artist: Martin Cross
Cover design: Duncan McTeer

First published 2002 by Folens Limited.

British Library Cataloguing in Publication Data. A catalogue record for this publication is available from the British Library.

ISBN 184303 244 9

ACKNOWLEDGEMENTS

Text extracts: 'Boy zone' by Geraldine Bedell from *The Observer*, 9 December 2001. © Geraldine Bedell, 2001; 'Monsters Inc.' from *The Guardian*, early 2002. © The Guardian; 'Car Safety – safe travel with your dog', published by the AA and the National Canine Defence League. Reproduced by permission of the AA and the National Canine Defence League; *Every Dog: A Complete Book of Dog Care* by Eric Allan and Rowan Blogg, published by OUP Australia; *The Naked Chef* by Jamie Oliver, published by Michael Joseph; 'Nothing's Changed' by Tatamkhulu Afrika; 'Island Man' by Grace Nichols from *The Fat Black Woman's Poems*, published by Virago; 'Two Scavengers in a Truck, Two Beautiful People in a Mercedes' by Lawrence Ferlinghetti, from *These Are My Rivers*, copyright © by Lawrence Ferlinghetti. Reprinted by permission of New Directions Publishing Corporation; 'Vultures' by Chinua Achebe from *Beware Soul Brother*, published by Heinemann Educational, reprinted by permission of David Bolt Associates on behalf of the author; 'What were they like?' by Denise Levertov from *Selected Poems*, published by Bloodaxe Books, reprinted by permission of Laurence Pollinger Ltd on behalf of the author and the proprietors, New Directions Publishing Corporation; 'Search For My Tongue' by Sujata Bhatt from *Brunizem* (1988) reprinted by permission of the publishers, Carcanet Press Limited; 'Unrelated Incidents' by Tom Leonard *from Intimate Voices: Selected Works 1965–1983*, published by Vintage; 'Half-Caste' by John Agard from *Get Back Pimple*, published by Penguin; 'Presents from my Aunts in Pakistan' by Moniza Alvi from *Carrying My Wife*, reprinted by permission of the publisher, Bloodaxe Books; 'Hurricane Hits England' by Grace Nichols from *Sunrise*, published by Virago; 'Riding High' from 2002 *Guinness World Records* edited by Antonia Cunningham. Copyright © Guinness World Records Limited; 'The Missing' by Dianne Taylor from *The Guardian*, 31 October 2001. © Dianne Taylor, 2001; 'The Tricks of the Trade' by Kathryn Flett from *The Observer*, 28 October 2001. © The Observer; *Immunisation: the safest way to protect your child*, published by the Health Education Authority. © Crown copyright, 1993; 'It's a Garage 'Ting' from *Message for the Media: Young Women Talk* edited by Jane Waghorn, published by Livewire, The Women's Press Limited; 'I'm used to dribbling, being thrown a dummy and cleaning up at the back' by Gary Mabbutt from *The Guardian*, 7 November 2001. © The Guardian; 'We went over the top' by Harry Patch from *The Guardian*, 8 November 2001. © Harry Patch, 2001; Extract from *Notes from a Small Island* by Bill Bryson, published by Black Swan, a division of Transworld Publishers. © Bill Bryson. All rights reserved.

Photographs: Paul Brown/REX features for page 40. Corbis for pages 59, 68, 80-81, 107, 124. Digital Vision for pages 17, 38, 39, 48, 56, 58, 63, 106, 119, 121, 128, 130. Ecoscene/Corbis for page 30. Getty Images for page 8. Suzanne Hubbard/REX features for page 76. Image State for pages 10 & 11. Nils Jorgensen/REX features for page 62. M Luft/REX features for page 126. Marcus Mays/REX features for page 122. Northern Rock advert pages 12 & 13 published courtesy of Cravens Advertising, Tim Morris - photographer and Northern Rock plc. Ann Pickford/REX features for page 49. Alexis Sofianopoulos/Ace photo agency for page 66. OMIKRON/SCIENCE PHOTO LIBRARY for page 98. Phanie/Alix/REX features for page 112. REX features for pages 10, 18, 19, 31, 33, 50, 72, 84, 108, 110, 115, 116, 129. PA Photos for p49. Peter Trievnor/REX features for page 116. Courtesy of Weider UK/Flex Magazine for page 143.

Illustrations: pages 90, 96: Brian Lee

CONTENTS

Contents

YOUR QUESTIONS ANSWERED

What exactly is a GCSE?

The letters stand for General Certificate of Secondary Education. GCSEs are available in almost every subject and most students finish them by the end of Year 11. Your GCSE results will be one of the most important factors in decisions you make about future education and employment.

Which GCSEs are available in the subject area of English?

English and English Literature.

What's the difference between them?

The English GCSE is based on four skills areas: speaking, listening, reading and writing. You will be assessed on a wide range of tasks that reflect the different kinds of English we use.

The English Literature GCSE is based on literary prose, poetry and drama. You will be assessed on your ability to understand and interpret literary texts from each of these three areas.

Will I need to do any coursework?

Coursework accounts for 40% of your grade in English and 30% of your grade in English Literature. It is made up of the following components.

English		English Literature	
Speaking and Listening	20%	Pre-1914 Drama	10%
Shakespeare	5%	Pre-1914 Prose	10%
Prose Study	5%	Post-1914 Drama	10%
Media	5%		
Original Writing	5%		
Total	**40%**		**30%**

Will I need to do exams?

Yes. The exam is worth 60% of your grade in English and 70% of your grade in English Literature. It is made up of the following components.

English		English Literature	
Paper 1 Section A	15%	Paper 1 Section A	35%
Paper 1 Section B	15%	Paper 1 Section B	35%
Paper 2 Section A	15%		
Paper 2 Section B	15%		
Total	**60%**		**70%**

Your questions answered

Is this a book about the GCSE English exam?

Yes. *Success in GCSE English for AQA/A* will help you prepare for the GCSE English exam. You will use other resources to help you with GCSE English coursework and with GCSE English Literature.

What will be in the GCSE English exam?

The GCSE English exam is an assessment of your reading and writing.

Paper 1 Section A	reading response to non-fiction and media texts
Paper 1 Section B	writing to argue, persuade and advise
Paper 2 Section A	reading response to poetry from different cultures and traditions
Paper 2 Section B	writing to inform, explain and describe

How long is the GCSE English exam?

Paper 1 is 1 hour and 45 minutes long. You will be advised to spend 1 hour on Section A and 45 minutes on Section B.

Paper 2 is 1 hour and 30 minutes long. You will be advised to spend 45 minutes on Section A and 45 minutes on Section B.

How is *Success in GCSE English for AQA/A* going to help me?

The book is written by teachers and examiners who will help you achieve the highest grade you possibly can. It will provide you with all the skills, knowledge and practice you need to prepare yourself fully for the GCSE English exam.

Key features:

- Page headers refer you to the relevant section of the exam.
- Units start with clear guidance on what will be covered.
- Large, bold numbering makes work easy to follow.
- Regular reference to key skills (red sub-headings) breaks learning into manageable 'chunks'
- Practice questions prepare you for the exam format.
- Examiner's Tips give advice on key points.
- Summaries at the end of each section provide main points for revision.

READING RESPONSE TO NON-FICTION/MEDIA TEXTS

In the next three units, you will:

- study a variety of different text types
- look at different texts on the same theme.

You will learn how to:

- interpret layout and visual images
- look at different texts on the same theme
- tell fact from opinion
- compare texts, identifying similarities and differences.

Introduction

The following three units deal with the 'reading response to non-fiction and media texts' section of the exam. In the exam, you will be presented with two or three linked non-fiction and media texts. You will have to answer a series of questions on them.

Where does this fit in the exam?

Paper 1 Section A

How long will I have?

You will have about an hour to complete the work.

How will these units help?

Each unit takes a different theme, such as 'Teenagers', and presents you with different texts around the theme. You will work through a variety of tasks on these texts, just as you will in the exam itself.

Read through this list of useful terms before you start this section.

article	a piece of non-fiction writing in a newspaper, magazine or book
bias	a prejudice for or against something or someone, which influences the way a text is written or constructed
collate	to bring together and compare
genre	a style of films, books, paintings, music etc, for example action adventure films, dance music
logo	an easily recognisable design used by an organisation in its publicity and advertising materials
masthead	the name of a newspaper or magazine as it appears in large print on the front cover
representation	the way in which a group of people, a place or an idea is depicted in the media
target audience	a particular group of people addressed or 'targeted' by a media text
web page	a page of information made accessible on computers through the World Wide Web

UNIT 1   FROM TEENAGERS TO YOUNG MEN

In this unit, you will focus on:

- a Sunday magazine article
- a building society advertisement.

1.1

Read the following views taken from a magazine article.

When you have read it, turn the page and look carefully at the advertisement produced for the Northern Rock Mortgage company.
Think about why it has been chosen for study alongside the article.

'I (Sam) was into hardcore bands like Limp Bizkit. But then everyone started liking hardcore, so now I've decided to go to more underground music, to make sure people won't find out about it. I listen mostly to modern punk rock, which is not as aggressive as the old punk rock.'

'I (Ben) get on well with them,' he says of his siblings. 'I sometimes go and stay with my sister, and I get quite a lot of stuff I like from my brother, like music. We both rap. I've got a kind of group with my friends... Timothy is amazing, all his family are: they all play drums and piano...Then there's Edwin, who's an old friend, and he's an amazing rapper too... We do deep raps and not-deep raps. Deep rapping is much more serious, but the other sort, a lot of it, is just boasting about how good we are, using metaphors... There's this rapper I really like... We stay swinging like a cowboy's lasso... Sticky fingers like UHU glue.'

All three boys spend quite a few of their evenings on the Internet, communicating with the people they have been with all day at school. Ntokozo admits that one of his favourite things is getting emails from girls: 'It's really cruel but I tend to reject the boys when the girls come on line. Some people have cussing matches, but mostly it's just gossip. We talk about who you like and who you don't like.' He thinks girls prefer boys who are funny.

Ntokozo's weekends are dominated by football: training on Saturdays, matches on Sundays. He plays at right back. 'The team's called Inter, I wasn't there when they named it… There's schoolboy football and there's football where you know what you're doing.' The [school] year team has never won a match.

Cedric says, 'I'm on the computer until 8pm. I play a lot of games – Driver 1 and 2, and Crash Bandicoot… and Streetfighter and Mortal Kombat. And I go on the Internet looking for top sites, and download ringtones and logos.' Cedric reckons that '90 to 95 per cent' of… pupils [in his year] have mobiles… friends at the local girls' school regularly send him messages saying things like, 'I'm in a maths lesson and it's really boring,' and (he) explained that 'texting has replaced passing notes, except you don't have to be in the same classroom.' He also, however, said that boys generally receive more than they send, because, 'it's so boring having to type it all out.' Cedric gets on well with his dad, despite his cluelessness about clothes. 'He doesn't know much. He tried to buy me these trainers called Ador… I like Adidas clothing, but clothes are just clothes. Everyone's different. What clothes you wear doesn't alter anything.'

Teenage boys are commonly treated as objects either of comedy or alarm… Adolescence has never been easy for boys, what with the acne pocking their faces, the voices that squeak and growl… But the less familiar aspects turn out to be incredibly appealing: the shyness and self-awareness, the mixture of childishness and remarkable sophistication. It is disconcerting that in the 21st century boys are still meant to grow up pretending to be invincible, but perhaps it's this that accounts for their charm: the rhinoceros hide conceals squidgy insides.

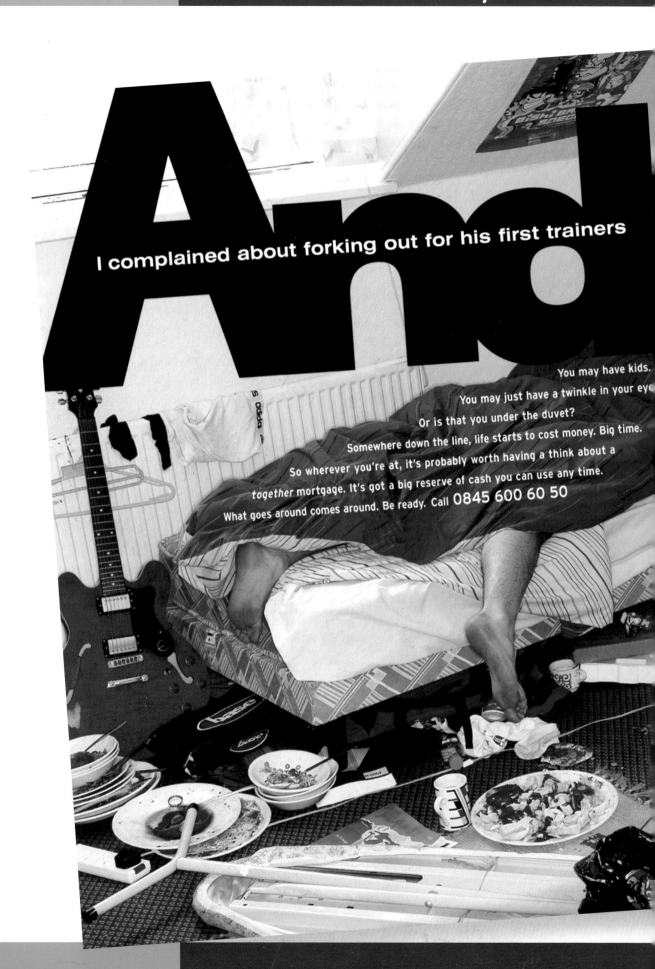

And

I complained about forking out for his first trainers

You may have kids.
You may just have a twinkle in your eye.
Or is that you under the duvet?
Somewhere down the line, life starts to cost money. Big time.
So wherever you're at, it's probably worth having a think about a
together mortgage. It's got a big reserve of cash you can use any time.
What goes around comes around. Be ready. Call 0845 600 60 50

Finding out what this part of the exam tests

When you are asked to compare two texts, you should comment on:

● how they are similar
● how they are different.

And, if they are 'media' texts, you are likely to have to comment on:

● visual presentation (where this is important)
● the language of the texts
● who they are aimed at (the audience)
● what their purpose is
(for example, to sell us something or to entertain us).

Let's deal with the article first, then the advertisement.

Knowing what a text is about

1.2 What is the main subject of the magazine article? Is it:

● fashionable music?   ● what matters to boys?
● playing football?   ● fashion and clothing?

If you're not sure, it's worth digging deeper.

1.3 To find out, draw a table like the one below and use the headings to write down what the boys have to say about each subject.

Subject	What the boys say
Music	
Rapping	
Computers and the Internet	
Families and parents	
Football	
Mobile phones	
Clothes	

It should now be pretty clear that the article is, in part, about how these boys enjoy spending their time. Write five or six sentences summarising what you have found out.

 Examiner's Tips

Notice how the boys' views are written in the first person, as if each boy is talking to the reader. There is little comment from the writer. This makes reading about the boys seem very personal.

Understanding the writer's purpose

.4 The writer of the article gives her opinions about teenage boys in the final paragraph of the article.

Write down four things that she claims are commonly said about teenage boys. The first one is done for you.

- *Objects of alarm*
-
-
-

Now write down which aspects of teenage boys' lives the writer claims are the most appealing.

.5 How have the writer's views about teenage boys changed as a result of writing the article about their lives?

> **You will need to cover the following points in your writing:**
>
> - what most people think of teenage boys
> - what the boys say about what they are interested in
> - what the writer now finds appealing about teenage boys.

> **Use these prompts if you wish:**
>
> - *Most people think that teenage boys are only interested in…*
> - *However, in the article, it shows that they like…*
> - *By the end, the writer feels that…*

.6 At the end of the unit, you will be asked to compare this article with the advert on pages 12 and 13. To prepare for this, go back to the article and think about:

>
> - whose 'voices' we hear in this article (just the boys?)
> - the sort of language used (is it formal? personal?).

Reading images

1.7

Look again at the Northern Rock advertisement.
Then close the pages.

> **Jot down what you remember about the advert:**
> - any objects
> - who, if anyone, was in it
> - the overall impression.
>
> Open the pages again.

Copy the table below, adding three more objects from the bedroom in each column.

Hobbies/Interests	Day-to-day living
science fiction poster	dirty cups

What impression does the advert give of young men? Take four objects from your table and explain how each adds to this impression.

For example: The science fiction poster suggests that young men are interested in stories about the future. It could also suggest that they like technology and travel.

1.8

Colour, and the way things are positioned (the composition) are also important and contribute to the general 'feel'.

Choose four words or phrases from this list which best describe the use of colour and composition in the advert.

> bright　　　busy　　confusing　　messy
> multi-coloured　　muddled　　untidy　　crowded

Now write two or three sentences explaining how the use of colour and composition in the advert add to the ideas about a young man's life.

1.9

The type of shot used can also add to the feel of the advert.

> **The photograph used in the advert is:**
> - a wide-angle shot
> - in sharp focus
> - brightly lit.

? Why do you think this is? Think about how the advert would have been different if the shot had been a close-up on one thing. What would have been lost?

Understanding how the written text is used

.10

There is not much text in the advertisement, but the way it is written and presented is important.

● The line 'And I complained about forking out for his first trainers' is in large letters and reads like part of a conversation.

? Who do you think is saying this line?

? Do you think it is said angrily, humorously or with affection?

'Or is that you under the duvet?'
The advert 'talks' to the reader as if he or she is a 'big kid'. Find three words or phrases that show this.

? How do the different lengths of sentence add to the impression of a young man's life?

.11

Who is this advert aimed at?

Consider these points
● it comes from the magazine section of a 'quality' weekend newspaper
● it is advertising mortgages
● it suggests a parent is speaking.

.12

The overall view

The advertisers seem to want to have a go at young men; it shows them as heavy drinkers, untidy, more interested in music and eating than in work or study. It is aimed at parents to say, if you were worried about trainers, you should be even more worried now!

If this is a picture of young men today, we should understand that this is meant as a light-hearted view. It is saying, this could be you – and there's nothing wrong with this, your mum and dad know exactly what's going on... as the main text at the top says. But, you might want to settle down one day with a girlfriend, and then you'll need us to help you buy your own place...

? Here are two candidates' responses to the advert. Which do you most agree with?

Comparing the two texts

The candidates on the previous page gave two different views of the advertisement. You may have different views to them.

In the exam, you will be asked to compare two texts (such as the advert and the article). In order to compare the texts, you need to look for both similarities and differences.

1.13   Compare the way young men's lives are presented in the advert, with the way that teenage boys' lives are presented in the extracts from a magazine article.

You will need to write about the following:

- what teenage boys themselves say about their interests
- what they enjoy doing
- the ways they spend their time
- what the writer of the magazine article thinks about teenage boys
- how the writer's views about teenage boys changed as a result of writing the article.

Look at your work on the magazine article on pages 14 and 15 to help you here.

You will need to write about the advert too, considering:

- what the advert is saying young men's lives are like
- how the images and presentation give this view
- how the writing gives this view.

How do you make comparisons between the two texts?

You can make these as you go along. In other words, you could make a comment about music in both texts (see opposite) and then go on to another topic.

Or you could wait until you have written about both texts, and then compare them.

Here is one student's response to task 1.13.

One way in which the advert and the magazine article are similar is that both place importance on music. In the advert, for example, there is a guitar in the bottom left hand corner. This suggests that young men are interested in playing music, particularly the guitar. In the magazine article the boys talk a lot about music. They like listening to it and also playing in bands.

However, one way in which the advert and the magazine article are different is that the advert has lots of dirty plates and cups on the floor which suggest that young men are very messy. In the magazine article the boys do not mention whether they are messy or not. If anything, their interest in fashion, and technology suggests...

Notice the words that the writer uses to help him or her compare:

● 'however' gives a different point of view
● 'suggests' is a good word for saying 'I think this means...'
● 'for example' tells the reader that the writer is going to provide 'evidence' to back up his or her point.

Now write your own comparison.
Use the bullet points in task 1.13 to guide you.

Remember:

● use comparison words (such as 'however', 'on the other hand', 'yet')
● use other organisational words (such as 'in addition', 'for example')
● use lots of examples (use the notes you have made)
● stick to the task (do not write about why building societies are boring!).

UNIT 2 MONSTERS: CLASSIC AND MODERN

In this unit, you will focus on:

- a movie preview booklet
- a magazine cover
- a web page.

Read this article from a 'movie preview' booklet. It was produced by *The Guardian* and *The Observer* newspapers and Buena Vista International UK Limited, a film company. Some written and presentational features have been pointed out, to help you to complete the tasks that follow.

Monsters, Inc
08/02/02

title of film and date of release

STILL 1

close-up shot of Sulley

information about the monsters

the main characters

Have you ever wondered what goes bump in the night? The new animated feature film Monsters, Inc reveals the monsters lurking in your bedroom cupboard while you sleep. But these are not your average monsters. Despite their frightening exterior, they have hearts of gold and are, in fact, only doing their job. They need to collect screams from children to power their parallel universe "Monstropolis".

Heading up the team at Monsters, Inc — the huge conglomerate at the heart of Monstropolis — is star scarer James P Sullivan ("Sulley").

This eight-foot hairy monster, voiced by the larger-than-life John Goodman, is proud that he is the company's scariest asset and takes its motto "We scare because we care" to heart.

With the help of diminutive one-eyed assistant Mike Wazowksi (Billy Crystal), he rules the Scare Floor, leaving all the other monsters, with the exception of Randall Boggs, in awe of his terror tactics.

Boggs (Steve Buscemi) is a slippery, slimy monster fed up with playing second fiddle to the ever popular Sulley. But he has a plan. He is going to ruin Sulley and take his place as the company's top scarer. He finally

Toy Story 2 was a tough act to follow but the team behind the hit have done it again

sees his chance when Sulley accidentally lets a little girl the monsters' world. This is bad news because legend h it in Monstropolis, that one touch from a human child i toxic to monsters.

What follows is a hyste chase as Sulley and Mike get the tiny tot back into h bedroom before Randall

STILL 2

low-angle shot on Sulley and little girl

names of directors and stars

STILL 3

long shot

STILL 4

mid shot

rector:
te Docter

Starring: John Goodman, Billy Crystal, Mary Gibbs,
Steve Buscemi, James Coburn, Jennifer Tilly

© DISNEY/PIXAR

links with other Disney
animations

hold of her for his own evil plot.
Toy Story 2 was a tough act to
follow but the team behind
the hit have done it again with
Monsters, Inc.
   Disney and Pixar have a
proven track record for their
highly original films, incredible
animation, lovable characters
and story lines that appeal to
children and adults alike.
   Monsters, Inc follows on in
the tradition of Toy Story and
A Bug's Life with a clever plot,
real-to-life animation, funny
one-liners and a whole host of
new characters in an adventure
that will have you laughing out
loud and reaching for your
hanky before the curtain is up.

'Monsters, Inc.
represents another
major achievement
for Pixar Animation
Studios and the art of
computer animation.
The film itself is a
brilliant piece of
entertainment
with memorable
characters and
hilarious situations'
THOMAS SCHUMACHER,
PRESIDENT OF WALT DISNEY
FEATURE ANIMATION STUDIOS

quotation from the president of
the studios

summary of the plot

Telling fact from opinion

Non-fiction texts, such as the *Monsters, Inc* preview you have just read, often rely on a clever mix of fact and opinion.

2.1

The words in large fonts at the top of each page draw the reader's attention to key facts or information.

Select and write down two facts and explain why each is important.

> The main text, however, tells readers more about the characters and storyline. In the last column, the writer gives opinions about the film.
>
> ● Select and write down three quotations which show that the writer thinks the film will be very successful.
>
> ● Explain in your own words what each quotation suggests about the film's main strengths or attractions.
>
> For example,
> The writer says: 'the team behind the hit (*Toy Story 2*) have done it again'.
> This suggests that *Monsters, Inc* is just as good as other Disney/Pixar productions.

Understanding the power of description

The following adjectives are used to describe the monsters:

frightening   scariest   hairy   diminutive

one-eyed   slippery   slimy   new

2.2

Check that you understand what each word means.

 What do these words tell us about the film and its characters?
Write two or three comments.

 Why might they make readers more interested in seeing the film? Explain in one or two sentences.

Interpreting visual images

Images are chosen very carefully in promotional texts. The position of the image, the size of it, who is in it, are all things that add to the point being made by the text – that the film is worth seeing.

2.3

The visual images are all 'stills' from the film. They have been numbered from 1 to 4.

● Copy and complete the following sentences about still 1, using the words in the blue box.

Still 1 is a close-up on Sulley. This makes us feel _____ with him.

It is a low-angle shot, so the camera is looking _____ at him.

This makes him seem _____.

His large white eyes and raised paws suggest that he is _____.

The main colour in this still is _____.

This colour is often used in horror or monster films. It can express _____

or _____.

Overall, this image makes the reader feel _____ towards Sulley.

frightened	sadness	bigger	up
cold	sympathetic	involved	blue

● Imagine that you were putting the review together. Pick one of the still images on page 21. Write down your reasons for using that particular image. Use the plan below.

Choice of image	I am very pleased that I picked still number _____ It is different from the other images because it shows _____.
Audience	Children would like this image because _____. It might also interest adults because _____.
Shot distance (long shot, mid shot or close-up)	It is a _____ shot. This means that readers can see _____
Camera angle (high or low)	I used a _____ camera angle. It makes the characters look _____.
Lighting	Lighting is used to draw attention to _____
Overall effects	I wanted to make readers feel _____ about the characters. I hoped that they would want to find out more about _____. I think this image will make audiences want to see Monsters, Inc because

Comparing two media texts

2.4 Study the web page and magazine cover on the next two pages.
Both texts refer to the 'horror' genre.

The *Monsters, Inc* website is designed to attract young Disney animation fans.
Classic Monsters magazine is about more 'serious' monsters in famous horror
films. Its target audience (the group of people it aims to attract) is film fans who
like old horror movies.

Comparing presentation and visual images

MONSTERS, INC.

Classic MONSTERS

The choice of fonts and logos is important in media texts.

2.5

Compare the *Classic Monsters* masthead (the name of the magazine, at the top of the page), and the *Monsters, Inc* logo displayed inside the central screen on the web page.

● Copy and complete the comparison below.

The _____ logo uses a round, friendly looking font. In the middle of the 'M', there is _____. This makes it look as though it is _____. _____. The _____ masthead is written in a big, irregular font to make it look _____. The 'M' seems to loom over you, which makes it more _____. They are both mainly _____, a colour often used in the horror genre.

2.6

Read what two students have written about the content and composition of these two texts.

Sara has noticed the following features of the *Monsters, Inc* web page.

There is a funny-looking machine that shows information about the film and how it was made.

The monsters are smiling and leaning on the machine.

The welcome message is right in the middle of the page.

The main colours are bright blues and greens and the background is white.

At the top of the page, there are red buttons.

For each of Sara's comments, write a sentence to explain how this makes the page more appealing to a young child.

For example, *The funny-looking machine shows that the film will be interesting, with lots of clever visual effects.*

Suhel writes about the composition of the *Classic Monsters* magazine cover.

I loved the feeling of a strange, unbalanced world where anything might happen.

I can tell immediately that this is about horror films.

The monsters look brilliantly dramatic and scary.

It gives the impression of a dark, night-time world.

For each of Suhel's comments, describe one visual feature that helps to give him this impression.

For example, *The strong diagonal line of the Frankenstein monster's arms makes the whole pa[ge] look unbalanced.*

Comparing written texts

.7

Look carefully at the words used in the two texts.

Choose two effective words or phrases from each text from the box below.
For each one, explain how it affected your response.

From the *Monsters, Inc* web page	From the *Classic Monsters* front page
'Welcome' 'Since the very first bedtime' 'View the new Outtakes' 'children around the world'	'Collectors' edition' 'Battle of the Titans' 'rare' 'behind the screams' (Tip: this is a pun, or word joke)

For example,

The web page uses the word 'Welcome'. It makes me feel that this site is open to anyone who is interested in the film.

.8

Use ideas from the work you have done on both texts
to answer this practice question.

Compare the representation of monsters in the web page and magazine front page.

Write one or two sentences about each of the following areas:

- visual similarities
- visual differences
- differences and similarities between the written texts
- the different target audiences for each text and how these affect the
  way the monsters are portrayed.

UNIT 3 — DOGS AND DOG CARE

In this unit, you will focus on:

- a leaflet
- a letter to a newspaper
- a non-fiction book.

Read the materials about dogs and their owners on the next three pages.

This leaflet is published by the National Canine Defence League and the AA, a motoring organisation. The labels point out how the writing (W), and layout, visual images and presentation (P), help to reinforce the advice given.
These labels will help you with task 3.5.

heading: emphasis on safety (W/P)

positive description of dog owners (W)

dog bones for bullet points (P)

bright, eye-catching yellow – the AA colour (P)

A safe journey

The NCDL and the AA, the leading experts in dog welfare and vehicle rescue, have produced this leaflet to prevent accidents to, or caused by, dogs in vehicles.

Dog owners in general care for their pets and look after them well. The object of this leaflet is to minimise those areas of inattention or thoughtlessness that can spoil the lives of the whole family. Hopefully, it will ensure that everyone enjoys their family outings and holidays.

Travel safely with your dog

- You are responsible for your dog's behaviour and safety.
- Use common sense.
- Treat your dog, in your car, as you would a small child.

Following these guidelines should ensure problem free and pleasant motoring for you, your family and your dogs.

imperative verbs (W)

funny cartoons to show dangers (P)

reasons given for advice (W)

subheading uses a pun (a word joke) (W)

bold text to draw attention to important fact (P)

insert showing safety cage (P)

attractive pictures of family dogs (P)

Safety when getting dogs into and out of a vehicle

🦴 Keep your dog controlled on a lead at all times when getting into or out of the car.

🦴 Never let your dog jump uncontrolled out of the car (or through the window!).

🦴 Make sure that it is **obvious to other motorists** that your dog is under control at all times.

Safety en route

🦴 Dogs should always travel on the back seat (or in the boot of estates and hatchbacks).

🦴 Always use a harness, dog guard or preferably a purpose built travel cage, even for short journeys, especially in open-top cars.

🦴 Make sure dogs cannot climb on or distract the driver.

🦴 Do not let your dog hang his head out of the window. It distracts other drivers and can damage his eyes – or worse!

🦴 Loose dogs in cars are as dangerous as an unsecured load if the vehicle has to stop

suddenly. 30lb of dog travelling at 80mph from the back to the front of the car will badly injure or even kill himself and other occupants.

Safety when leaving a dog (or dogs) in the car

🦴 If your dog is required by law to be muzzled **in public** it must be muzzled in your car. A car parked in a public place is regarded by law as a **public place**.

🦴 An unsecured dog left alone in a stationary vehicle can cause injury to himself and damage to the car. Always leave him secured in the rear in a harness/behind a dog guard or in a purpose built travel cage.

Hot Dogs in Cars

🦴 Never leave your dog in a car in hot weather for longer than 5 minutes. It can result in the dog's death and/or your prosecution.

Even with the windows open, the temperature can quickly reach 95°F (35°C). Your dog can suffer from heat-stroke within 20 minutes (or less!) of being left in the car.

How to avoid your dog suffering from heat-stroke:

🦴 **NEVER** leave your dog in the car in warm weather.

🦴 **AVOID** taking your dog on long car journeys in hot weather.

🦴 If a long journey is essential, provide plenty of water and stop frequently for fresh air.

A letter to the *Eastside Gazette*

Dirty Dogs

I am writing to express my disgust about the growing problem of dog mess in our local streets. It seems to have got worse every year, and it's time something was done about this menace.

Every morning, I walk my two young children to school. This used to be a pleasant experience. But nowadays, we are forced to play hopscotch in order to avoid the smelly piles of waste littered all over our pavements. On two occasions recently, my little boy has arrived at school having stepped in one of these piles. The teachers have dealt with this situation very well, but really it is not their job to clean my son's shoes because of the inconsiderate behaviour of dog owners. These people have no concern for the health and safety of local children.

There are laws about controlling your dog in the street. Dog owners should carry a scoop and a suitable plastic bag when walking their pets. The Council has tried to make this easier; there are at least two dog waste bins in the streets surrounding the school. But no one ever uses these. The law should be enforced.

I do not want to live in a dog toilet, and I'm sure that my views are shared by many. So wake up, dog owners! Clean up your act! A well-trained dog is everyone's best friend... but only if it's properly cared for.

Gail Barker (Mrs)

An extract from *A Complete Book of Dog Care*

Problem Behaviour

Surveys disagree on precise numbers, but the startling fact remains that over 20 per cent of dogs have behaviour problems significant enough to disrupt their owners' normal life or routine. These unsocial activities rarely cause the dog itself any inconvenience or pain; however, they are hard for others to tolerate.

The most frequent complaint is aggressive behaviour, such as biting or attacking, but other common problems include excessive barking and objectionable sexual behaviour such as mounting and urine spraying, or destructiveness, phobias, and roaming or escaping.

In many cases, the owners of these dogs do little or nothing to correct the problem, even if it seriously disrupts their lives. For example, owners of aggressive dogs sometimes find that friends stop visiting them, or they cannot allow other children to visit. In other cases, owners of dogs which bark hysterically when left alone cease to go out much. Others no longer go away for their holidays because their pet frets too much or becomes destructive.

Many of these problems can be controlled, and early recognition of their existence will allow you to start a correction programme before the behaviour becomes established. Results are far better with problems of recent origin than with longstanding, deeply ingrained habits.

A better understanding of the workings of a dog's mind helps to clear some of these misconceptions. There is an almost universal tendency to try to translate our dogs' behaviour into human terms such as guilt, selfishness, bullying, vindictiveness, and so on. A dog has none of these sensitivities. It cannot tell right from wrong.

A dog which has chewed up the lounge cushions in the owner's absence will usually act in a cowed and submissive way when the owner discovers its deed. Naturally, we interpret this as guilt. In fact, the answer is simpler. The dog is anticipating punishment – it is fear that it feels. Perhaps it is the owner's body language that triggers this response, or perhaps the dog has learned to associate the presence of a lot of debris with punishment. Whatever the emotion, it is not guilt. The destruction will occur again unless the owner finds and eliminates the reason for it. Punishment at this stage is too late, as the dog does not and cannot connect the misdeed with the punishment. Punishment will only make him become more anxious and therefore more prone to problem behaviour.

Many owners claim that their dog understands everything they say. In fact, a dog never understands more than a fraction of our vocabulary, although some dogs comprehend up to 50 or so words. However, dogs are extremely good at reading gestures and expressions, and other ways of communicating, such as tone of voice or even habits and routine. They may not understand the words you say, but they know what you mean.

If you want to understand your dog better, try not to think of him as a human. By all means shower him with affection and attention, but do not expect him to think or react as you do. Some knowledge of the behaviour of your dog's background and his ancestor – the wolf – may help you to understand him better.

Selecting appropriate material and following arguments

Each of the texts about dogs deals with them in a different way. They provide:

- information in different ways
- different mixes of fact and opinion
- different layouts and styles of presentation
- their own viewpoints.

Let's look at each text in turn.

3.1 Turn to the leaflet 'A Safe Journey' on pages 28–29.

- Select and write down three ways in which dog owners can protect their pets from damage or injury on a car journey.
- Explain in your own words why the writers of the leaflet believe that keeping your dog safe in the car will mean a safe journey for everyone.

? Are these facts or opinions – or a mix of both?

3.2 Read the extract on 'Problem Behaviour' on page 31.

According to the writer, what mistakes do dog owners make in managing their dogs?
(Tip: several mistakes are mentioned in paragraph 3.)

Start your answer like this:
One mistake owners make is to do little or nothing to correct a problem. Another is...

3.3 Now reread the letter to a local paper, 'Dirty Dogs' on page 30.

- Select and write down two quotations which express Mrs Barker's feelings about the behaviour of dog owners.
- For each quotation, find and write down in your own words a fact from the letter which backs up her point or helps to explain why she feels so strongly.

For example,
Mrs Barker says 'I am writing to express my disgust'. This is explained by the fact that her little boy has arrived at school twice with dirty shoes because there is so much dog mess on the pavement.

Identifying similarities and differences between texts

Now compare the book extract, 'Problem Behaviour', with the letter to the paper, 'Dirty Dogs'.

> **Compare the ways the two writers criticise dog owners.**
>
> **Write about:**
> ● the purpose and audience for each text
> ● what each writer says about dog owners
> ● the language they use
> ● how they try to convince readers that their views should be acted on.

Use these starters if you wish. Write three sentences on each bullet point.

● The book, *A Complete Book of Dog Care* is written for people who already own a dog. Its purpose is to help them to look after their dogs...

● The writer of the book says that dog owners do not always understand their pets very well, because...

● The letter is written in strong, critical language to show how angry the writer is. For instance...

● The writer of the book uses facts to show that her ideas are sound. One example is...

Commenting on a media text

Reread the leaflet , 'A Safe Journey'.

> **Use the points around the leaflet to help you to answer the questions below.**
>
> ● How does the written text encourage readers to follow the advice given?
> ● How do layout, visual images and presentation help to make the advice clear and friendly?

Practice questions

The following questions look back over the texts you have studied in units 1, 2 and 3. Make sure you reread all the relevant texts.

Remember that the key skills you must demonstrate are:

- looking at different materials on the same theme or subject matter
- following arguments or viewpoints
- selecting appropriate material to write about
- identifying differences and similarities between texts.

Questions on the magazine article extracts and the Northern Rock advert

---

Read the magazine article about teenage boys on pages 10–11.
You are being asked to select and collate appropriate material.

1. Write down **three** activities that the boys are most interested in.   (3 marks)

2. Choose **three** examples of language from the magazine article and explain how the language used makes teenage boys' lives appear exciting and interesting.
   (6 marks)

Now read the advert from the Northern Rock on pages 12–13.

3. What additional information about young men's lives is included in this advert? Choose **three** details and explain how each is similar or different to the magazine article.   (6 marks)

You are now being asked to read the advert as a media text.

4. How does the layout and presentation of the advert help you to understand the view of young men's lives being presented?   (6 marks)

5. Choose **three** examples of language used in the advert and explain how each is appealing to adults who have experience of teenage boys.   (6 marks)

Total: 27 marks

Questions on *Monsters, Inc* movie preview and web page

Read the *Monsters, Inc* movie preview on pages 20–21.
You are being asked to follow an argument and select appropriate material.

1. Write down the names of three characters mentioned in the preview.

   (3 marks)

2. Explain in your own words the part each character plays in the team at
   Monsters, Inc. How is each character important in the storyline?

   (6 marks)

Now read the *Monsters, Inc* web page on page 24.
You are being asked to compare the preview and web page as media texts.

3. Choose **three** examples of language from the preview and explain how each
   example makes the film sound exciting and interesting.   (6 marks)

4. Choose **three** examples of language used on the web page and explain how each
   example shows that the film and web page are suitable for family viewing.

   (6 marks)

5. Compare the use of images and layout in the preview and web page. What are the
   similarities and differences in the way that each text presents its information?

   (6 marks)

Total: 27 marks

**Questions on the materials about dogs: 'A Safe Journey',
'Dirty Dogs' and 'Problem Behaviour'**

Read the book extract, 'Problem Behaviour' on page 31.
You are being asked to follow an argument and select appropriate material.

1. Write down **three** examples of dogs' behaviour problems mentioned in the extract.

   (3 marks)

2. Look at the sixth paragraph.
   Explain in your own words why the writer thinks that it is wrong to say that dogs
   feel guilt after they have behaved badly.   (6 marks)

**Now look at the leaflet, 'A Safe Journey' (pages 28–29), and the letter,
'Dirty Dogs' (page 30). You are being asked to compare the two texts and to
identify facts and opinions.**

3. Select **three** facts from each text. Explain how each fact is used to back up the
   writer's opinions about the right way to look after a dog.   (9 marks)

Now look at the leaflet, 'A Safe Journey' as a media text.

4. What are the main purposes of this leaflet?   (3 marks)

5. How has the leaflet been written, designed and laid out to appeal to
   dog owners?

   (6 marks)

Total: 27 marks

SUMMARY

- For any text you are asked to read, think carefully about the audience
  and purpose.

  ? In other words, who was it written for? What does
  the writer want to get them to think or do?

- Remember to look out for facts and opinions.

- Identify layout and presentational devices. Work out how each of these helps
  to address the audience and purpose of the text.

WRITING TO ARGUE, PERSUADE AND ADVISE

Introduction

The following three units will develop the writing skills required for one of the two writing sections of the exam. In the exam, you will have a choice of writing questions using these text types.

Where does this fit in the exam?

Paper 1, Section B

How long will I have?

You will have about 45 minutes to complete the work.

How will these units help?

Each unit deals with one of the text types in turn.

Read through this list of useful terms before you start this section.

anecdote
a short, personal story of something that happened to you or someone you know; sometimes useful to make your advice seem more real and interesting

audience
the readers you aim to attract to your ideas

brainstorming
writing down all your first ideas, however good or bad you think they are – later, you can choose which ones to use

connectives
words or phrases that make links between your ideas, for example, 'first', 'next', 'however', 'on the other hand'

imperative verb
a verb that tells someone what to do, for example, '*Look* over there!', '*Be* careful'

purpose
the reason for producing a piece of writing – what you hope to gain or achieve

relevant points
ideas or points that are closely linked to the topic on which you are giving advice

rhetorical question
a question which doesn't require an answer and is used to make a point, for example 'Who's going to win the League, then?'

topic sentence
the first sentence of a paragraph; it tells the reader what the paragraph is about

WRITING TO ARGUE

In this unit, you will:

- explore some of the skills needed when you write to argue a point
- study a newspaper article which gives different points of view about Hallowe'en
- write your own article about children's eating habits in primary schools.

You will learn how to:

- give reasons for a point of view
- collect and link your ideas together
- use techniques in your writing to develop the point of view and argument.

One key thing to remember:

- Writing to argue can compare opinions or points of view in order to get its message across.

A point of view is an opinion that someone feels strongly about. It is often backed up with reasons in order to explain it.

Expressing a point of view

.1

Here two students give their opinions about homework being set for the weekend.

I hate it when a teacher says 'I'm going to leave setting you your homework until Friday because then you will have three nights and two days to complete it and will be able to produce your best possible work'. I mean, don't teachers realise that I have a life? I usually go out with my mates on Friday night and I work on Saturdays. On Sunday mornings I stay in bed recovering from all my hard work. I really think I deserve some relaxation and pleasure in my life.

I much prefer being given my homework to do at the weekends, it gives me much more choice about when I do it. I can decide whether to do it during the day or in the evenings. During the week you don't get this choice as homework usually has to be completed in the evening for the next day. I'm usually very tired in the evenings as I belong to a diving club and we meet three times a week to practise.

 What reasons have each of the pupils given?
Do you think they are valid?

 Which of the two points of view do you most agree with?

1.2

Read the following article. Look at the features used by the writer to argue a number of points about Hallowe'en.

the title tells you the focus of the article – it uses rhyme: 'fright' and 'night'

paragraph 1 tells a story and presents Benjamin enjoying Hallowe'en

the sub-heading asks a question – this will be answered in the article

FRIGHT AT NIGHT

Is Hallowe'en too scary for young children?

the third person

It is Hallowe'en night and three-year-old Benjamin is already asking if he can go 'trick or treating' with his nine-year-old sister and seven-year-old brother. He has already dressed himself in a face mask covered in glitter, which he has made at nursery, and a black bin liner to match the one worn by his brother. Also, he has already visited the house next door and in the warmth of the kitchen tucked into jelly skulls and missing finger sweets. So when there is a knock at the front door, Benjamin rushes to answer it.

the active voice – it describes what Benjamin is doing

However, when he sees five children dressed in monster masks and crowding around the door opening yelling, 'Hallowe'en, trick or treat?' Benjamin runs to hide behind his mother's legs in order to hand over the chocolate treats. When there comes a second, third and then fourth knock, Benjamin refuses to go anywhere near the door and in fact hides behind the curtains. Later in bed he is too scared to sleep alone and that night sleeps with his parents. On the other hand his brother and sister have had a great time!

paragraph 2 also tells the story of Benjamin but shows him scared by Hallowe'en

a connective – it joins the paragraphs together

the present tense – as though it is happening now

paragraph 3 explains why Hallowe'en is scary for young children

expert opinion to support the writer's viewpoint

According to an article in the *Guardian* newspaper, most children love Hallowe'en. But for young children the experience can be traumatic. A social psychologist has said that while people dressed up as monsters or ghosts are figures of fun to adults because adults know they are not real, young children do not know this. Young children do not understand the difference between what is pretend and what is real.

paragraph 4 continues to explain why Hallowe'en is scary

In addition to this, some nursery teachers believe that four year olds are usually afraid of monsters and ghosts. They keep this fear until they are about seven although they are able to rationalise it a little from the age of five years. Thus it would appear that for Benjamin the incident at the door could have been traumatic; for him the masks were real.

paragraph 5 gives a different viewpoint – it says Hallowe'en can be a useful experience

a connective phrase shows the viewpoint is changing

On the other hand, it has also been pointed out, by an educational psychologist, that for older children Hallowe'en can be a useful way to teach them about confronting their own fears. He believes that once children are able to rationalise their own fears, and recognise that the monsters at the door are not real, then they may well be scared but not frightened. Dealing with fear is a necessary part of growing up.

paragraph 6 summarises the two viewpoints and gives a final opinion

So looking at the experience of one three year old it is important to remember that if you celebrate Hallowe'en with small children you check that the frights are not too frightening and the ghosts are not too ghostly. Hallowe'en is a different experience for a three year old and a seven year old.

the final sentence

use of second person to encourage the reader to identify

This article:
- is written in six paragraphs
- gives two different views about Hallowe'en
- opens with a story to introduce the ideas
- finishes with a summary of the two views and a final opinion.

Using connectives

Connectives are words that can help to build an argument.
Here are three of the many ways in which they can be used:

● to add to the argument
Example: Another point I want to make is…

● to support the argument
Example: As expert, Professor Perkins, says...

● to introduce a new viewpoint (which might be argued against later).
Example: In contrast there is evidence that…

1.3

Look at these connective words.

> **Decide which:**
>
> ● adds information to a viewpoint
> ● supports it
> ● introduces a new viewpoint.

However…   **According to…**   **On the other hand…**

Additionally…   **Despite this…**   **Moreover…**   **Supporting this…**

Writing in paragraphs

Paragraphs help to make sense of your ideas and to link them together.

> **Remember:**
>
> ● Start a new paragraph when you write about something new or different.
> ● The first sentence of a new paragraph can be linked in some way to the previous paragraph.

1.4

Have a look at the way the writer of the article on Hallowe'en begins
paragraphs 3 and 4. Make a note of the first two words in each paragraph.

 Do these paragraphs add to a viewpoint, support it,
or introduce a new viewpoint?

Using evidence and quotation

It is important to use evidence to make your arguments stronger.
Evidence may come from:

● experts

● personal experience

● books, data, etc.

Sometimes people's actual words are used. These are called quotations.

.5 Read through the article on Hallowe'en again and identify the different types of evidence mentioned above.

> **?** Do these forms of evidence affect your opinions?

Using questions

Questions can be used to:

● create a dialogue with the reader

● make the reader feel the writer knows the answers.

.6 Look again at the article about Hallowe'en. The question in this article appears as the sub-heading.

'Is Hallowe'en too scary for young children?'

Write down:

● one reason why the writer believes Hallowe'en is scary for young children

● one reason why Hallowe'en is not scary for older children.

Deciding in which 'person' to write

Remember:

● First person talks about 'I'. It makes an argument very personal.

● Third person talks about 'he', 'she', 'they' etc. The writer does not mention him or herself. It makes the argument seem fair and well argued.

.7 Look through the article on Hallowe'en and see if you can find any examples of the writer using the first person, mentioning him or herself.

Crafting your own argument

Read this question. It invites you to argue your point of view.

'Should we be controlling what our children eat?'

Work through the tasks. Some of the work has been done for you.

1.8 An opening sentence and first paragraph

Read this example, which:

● is written in the present tense
● tells the story of one child.

Amy opens her lunch box every day and takes out her tomato sandwich, cheese and onion crisps, some olives, a yoghurt and a banana. First she eats her yoghurt as she doesn't want it to get any warmer, then she eats her sandwich with her crisps and olives. She finishes with her banana. If she looks around she will see other children tucking into their lunches but what she will not see are any children eating chocolate or sweets. The school has banned them from the dining hall.

Now write your own first sentence and paragraph describing the eating habits of a particular child. You could start:

... opens his/her lunch box and ...

Writing to argue

9

A question

The second paragraph must link with the first paragraph and could cover what parents think.
This is going to be done using a question.

> **Choose one of the questions below, or write your own:**
>
> ● Can you believe how happy parents are?
> ● Are parents complaining to the school about this healthy change?

The paragraph continues:

Parents of the children welcome the decision the school has taken as it means that the children are being encouraged to eat in a healthy way and not fill themselves up with a lot of sweets.

Comments or quotations

Quoting someone's actual words will add interest and weight to your argument.
Copy and complete the sentence:

One parent commented, 'My son Kyle wouldn't ever eat fruit; he prefers...'

New information or evidence

The third paragraph will give evidence about healthy eating.
It will use evidence from a dentist who encourages healthy eating because it is good for children's teeth.

Write down one or two sentences that the dentist might say.

What is more, the school dentist, Ms Khan, says that...

1.12   A contrasting viewpoint

This can now be introduced. It will suggest that the school has no right to say what children eat. It must begin with a connective to show that the paragraph is going to give a different point of view.

> **Decide which of the following openings you would use in your writing:**
>
> ● Even though there is a lot of evidence in favour of healthy eating...
>
> ● However, even though there is a lot of evidence...
>
> ● Despite all this evidence in favour of healthy eating...
>
> ● On the other hand, some people feel that the school is...

Complete the paragraph, adding reasons why the school should have no right to say what children eat at lunchtime.

1.13   Completing the argument

> **The final paragraph needs to:**
> ● review and summarise all the views discussed
> ● finish with an interesting sentence.

Here is how it could be written.

Thus it is important, when considering all the views about whether eating sweets and chocolate should be allowed in schools at lunchtime, that the interests of the pupils are considered first. A child who does not eat in a healthy way may need encouragment to eat fruit and vegetables but a child who already eats fruit and vegetables, may be all right with a lunchtime bar of chocolate. What is important is that pupils, parents and the school maintain a balanced view and diet. After all, you are what you eat!

.14 Use the skills developed in this unit to answer this practice question.

Write an article for a school magazine in which you argue for or against pupils being allowed to come to school with body piercing and studs.

You could consider the following areas in your argument:

- the personal experience of yourself or a friend or relation
- where body piercing and studs normally show
- the reasons why school pupils like or dislike body piercing and studs
- the views and rules of the school
- parents' opinions of these views and rules
- your opinion of these rules and views
- your recommendations.

Examiner's Tips

Show that you are aware of at least two opinions that are opposite to your own. Show that you can see some good in them before dismissing them.

SUMMARY

- You can put forward another argument, before knocking it down.
- Use plenty of connectives, such as 'however' or 'so', to guide your argument.
- If you can, use evidence and/or quotations.
- Finish by summarising your main argument in a clear way.

UNIT 2 WRITING TO PERSUADE

In this unit, you will:

- explore some of the skills needed when you are writing persuasively
- read and study an article written by a student teacher.

You will learn how to:

- get your readers interested in your ideas
- convince them that what you say is true, or that they should do what you say.

One key thing to remember:

- writing to persuade emphasises one main opinion.

Identifying purpose and audience

2.1 Read the two extracts below.

> **For each extract, identify**
> - the audience (who is the writer talking to?)
> - the purpose (what does he/she want them to think or do?)

Voting for me as your local Monster Raving Loony Party candidate will make a real difference to the lives of everyone in this borough. Do you seriously think the major political parties have the slightest interest in local issues? For instance, have they ever put up any funny road signs in sparkly colours? Have they bothered to declare your area a Dinosaur Free Zone? Of course they haven't. They're far too busy writing boring rules and regulations and having all-night parties in the Houses of Parliament. Do they ever invite you to these parties? I think not. So think very carefully before you cast your vote.

Tired of all those beauty products that promise you a face fit for Hollywood, but end up making no difference at all?

Try Wizviz Beauty Capsules and you'll soon see a difference. Your friends will wonder what's the secret of your new, beautiful looks – because Wizviz capsules contain unique beauty-enhancing ingredients which work from the inside out. So you know that every day, you're growing more beautiful the healthy way.

2.2

Now try out your own persuasive powers.

Remember what it's like when you have a new teacher, one your class has never met before?

Work with a partner.

> ● Your **audience** is the new teacher.
> ● Your **purpose** is to try to persuade him or her to give you a really easy time!

Write down two or three things you might say. Remember that the new teacher is no fool. You'll have to back up your points with some powerful persuasion!

Here are some examples to get you going:

Miss, the Head of Year told us that we each have to chew at least three packets of gum every day, to keep our teeth nice and healthy. It's really hard work – but we'll be in such trouble if we don't keep up with our targets.

Miss, our old teacher only set homework once every three weeks. She said that scientists at the University of Cambridge have proved that we learn better that way.

Now listen carefully to your partner's ideas.

2.3

Read the chart below.

Think of two more reasons why the second example is effective.
Complete the final two bullets on the list.

Persuasive argument	Why is it effective?
Example 1 "Miss, our old teacher only set homework once every three weeks. She said that scientists at the University of Cambridge have proved that we learn better that way."	● It makes the new teacher think that you know more than she does about the school's homework policy ● It makes her think that your idea is backed up by clever experts from a well known university ● It makes her feel that she is being less kind and less effective than the previous teacher
Example 2 "Miss, the Head of Year told us that we each have to chew at least three packets of gum every day, to keep our teeth nice and healthy. It's really hard work – but we'll be in such trouble if we don't keep up with our targets."	● Uses an authority figure – the Head of Year – to back up the argument ● ●

Now sketch a similar chart with the same headings and add your arguments and those of your partner.

Say why each argument was effective.

After you have filled in the chart, discuss which of the arguments would be most likely to succeed.

2.4

Read this persuasive text by a trainee teacher. She is trying to persuade a class to behave well. Does it work?

As you read, look at the labels which show how she has tried to make her writing convincing and persuasive. Some of the techniques are the same or similar to those you might use to argue or to advise – see how many of these you can spot.

TREAT YOUR TRAINEE TEACHER RIGHT

It's a rainy Monday morning, period one, English. To be honest, you would much rather be snuggling under your warm duvet than preparing to analyse *Romeo and Juliet*. However, as you enter your English classroom, you see a new face.

Someone you don't know is reading the poetry wall display at the back of the room. She greets pupils with a quiet 'Good Morning'. Great, a trainee teacher, nervous and uncertain. Suddenly, the morning seems interesting.

Now, if you're thinking that this provides an opportunity to brighten up your lesson with some harmless trainee teacher torturing, think again. In fact, as you sit down at your desk and take out your books, think again of four very important reasons why you should be pleasant to Miss Trainee Teacher:

- The trainee teacher (we'll call her T.T.) is at your school to learn and improve her teaching skills. Your regular teacher is also her teacher and T.T. is keen to impress them. So keen that if you ask her to help you, she will bend over backwards to do so. The weekend is over so why not take advantage of T.T.'s willingness to make your morning easier?
- T.T. has also spent the past fortnight making sure that she knows *Romeo and Juliet* like the back of her hand. Fantastic – more brains for you to pick when your regular teacher is busy with pupils at the other end of the classroom.
- After spending several weeks in your school, it's possible that T.T. will be asked to join the teaching staff permanently. T.T. could be your full-time teacher or form teacher this time next year. So, think of your kindness to her as a long-term investment!
- … And the most important reason why you should treat T.T. with a little respect? Well, it's because you are a friendly, polite and altogether mature secondary school pupil of course. How lucky T.T. is to be teaching you!

Labels:

- imperative instruction sounds confident
- first, main argument
- development: further reasons
- short, punchy sentence to end
- use of second person makes reader feel involved
- rhetorical question
- connectives pull argument together
- humorous end, flatters reader

Planning and writing with purpose and audience in mind

Below is the first draft of a bike shop advertisement.

'Wheel World Bikes' are planning to place their advert in a wide range of magazines during November and December.

> Their *purpose* is to try to get parents to buy a new bike for their child for Christmas.
>
> Their target *audience* is the parents or carers in families that celebrate Christmas. But they also want their advert to appeal to children who might see it. So, there are two audiences.

Come to Wheel World this Christmas

- We have all the best bikes from around the world.

- We also stock a wide range of cycling clothes and equipment.

- We're always up to date. For instance, we now have in the new solar-powered Uphill Racer snake-board. Free trial rides are available on our indoor Worm-hole Flume (admission for over-11s only).

- All our bikes are safety checked by WW mechanics. They carry an optional 3-year warranty. And you can benefit from our experts' advice on bike choice and bike safety.

- Wheel World has the biggest range of bikes and equipment in town, AND we offer the most competitive prices.

Don't dream of going anywhere else – come to WW for the bike of your dreams!

2.5 Write down three ways in which the advert already appeals to its audiences – parents/carers and children.

Using expressive language

2.6

Expressive language has a persuasive effect on the reader.

The first bullet point in the draft advert on page 53 is written in rather plain language.

Here's how another writer made the first sentence more expressive.
Pick out the words or phrases he has used to make you feel impressed:

We have a stunning collection of bikes from every corner of the globe

Now improve the second bullet point.

If you like, you can add one or two extra sentences.

Make your readers feel that they will look great and feel well equipped if they buy products from Wheel World.

You could start like this:

But Wheel World doesn't just stock bikes. You can get into gear with our brilliant selection of...

Using a variety of arguments or reasons

This will help to make your persuasive writing stronger.

2.7

Look at the points already suggested. With a partner, write down two or three extra points to get families to buy their presents at Wheel World.

> **You could base these on:**
> ● why Christmas is a good time to buy your child a new bike
> ● how well known the shop is
> ● special deals or offers.

Addressing your readers directly

Here's how the third bullet point from the advert could be developed.

The writer now seems to be talking more directly to the teenage audience.

- We have all the best bikes from around the world.

- We also stock a wide range of cycling clothes and equipment.

Wheel Crazy!

- We're always up to date with the latest crazes. Reserve your solar-powered Uphill Racer snake-board before anyone else does. Or, how about a free trial ride on our thrilling indoor Worm-hole Flume? (Admission for steely-nerved over-11s only!)

- All our bikes are safety checked by WW mechanics. They carry an optional 3-year warranty. And you can benefit from our experts' advice on bike choice and bike safety.

- Wheel World has the biggest range of bikes and equipment in town, AND we offer the most competitive prices.

2.8

Reread the new version above.

Identify where the writer has:

- added a snappy sub-heading
- introduced the idea of 'crazes': this makes the shop sound more in touch with teenagers' interests
- used an imperative: this might encourage readers to do what is suggested
- appealed to the readers' wishes to seem up to date and brave
- used a rhetorical question
- used a persuasive adjective.

2.9   Now reread the fourth bullet point on the original advertisement. Rewrite it, making it appeal more directly to parents and carers.

You could start like this:

Parents! Of course you want to make sure your child is really safe on that new...

2.10   Complete the advert.

Turn the first draft into a whole-page advert for Wheel World's Christmas offers.

- Write around 200 words. Think carefully about layout and presentation (revise the ideas on these areas covered in the units on Paper 1 Section A).

- Apply all the skills you have learned to each part of the original draft. Add some of your own ideas if you want.

- If you have access to a computer, you could add graphics and other effects. Look at real examples of bike adverts for inspiration.

2.11   **Use the skills developed in this unit to answer this practice question.**

Write a flier to put through local people's doors, advertising a big open-air music and comedy show. The show will be taking place in a park or open space in your area.

Include:

- the reasons why this will be an unmissable experience
- some tantalising examples of the acts and performers
- arguments to suggest that the show will offer good value for money
- reassurance to older people that the show won't create too much noise and litter
- a special offer for local people who apply early for tickets.

Examiner's Tips

Use expressive language to make the show sound exciting. Use the bullet points to guide you in adding several reasons. Aim to interest different audiences.

SUMMARY

- Use a variety of reasons to show that your view is right.
- Flatter your reader.
- Use rhetorical questions and humour (if appropriate).
- Use expressive/powerful language.
- Have a strong ending.

UNIT 3 WRITING TO ADVISE

In this unit, you will:

- look at advice given to young children on how to learn the basics of using a kitchen
- read a recipe for chocolate tart, written by Jamie Oliver, TV's 'Naked Chef'
- practise writing your own advice for different audiences.

You will learn how to:

- collect and organise relevant points
- write clear, helpful advice in the right tone
- hold the interest of your readers or audience.

One key thing to remember:

- writing to advise requires a clear and firm tone that is not bossy.

Using imperative verbs

Written advice often contains imperative verbs.
These tell your reader what to do and what not to do.

3.1

Below is some advice for people planning a holiday on the Moon!

Moondream Holidays are delighted to welcome you on the very first Out Of This World Safari! Here are some tips to help you to get the most out of your week.

Take a camera or camcorder to record magic moments during your holiday.

Pack lots of light clothes to wear in your air-conditioned hotel.

Sign up for a buggy ride across the Moon's famous craters.

Keep awake during that unforgettable shuttle ride.

Don't drop litter on the Moon.

Remember to send postcards to all your friends back on Earth!.

● Write down five imperative verbs used in this advice.

Write your own list of holiday Dos and Don'ts for one of the holidays below.

● 'Learn to Surf' week in Newquay
● School geography trip
● City Break in a city of your choice
● Clubbers' weekend in Spain

3.2

Read this example of some written advice. It comes from a book written for children aged between eight and eleven. Discuss how the writer has tried to make her ideas appeal to young children.

Ready, Steady, Get Cooking!

Do you like the look of some of the scrumptious recipes pictured in this book? Are you nearly ready to get cooking? Here are some handy hints to make sure that you have a really good time in the kitchen.

Get Ready!

Before you start cooking, **check that an adult in your house or flat knows what you are doing**. Make sure that they are happy to be around and lend a hand if you need one, and to make sure that you are cooking safely.

Good chefs set a shining example, so **always give your hands a good wash** before you start. One of the joys of cooking is the pleasure you'll see on your friends' or family's faces when they try your yummy dishes. Nobody wants to eat grey pudding! You can also keep yourself and your clothes clean when you are in the kitchen by **wearing an apron**.

To get completely ready, **check through your recipe** and make sure that you understand everything. You can always ask someone if there's anything you're not sure about. Next, **get together everything that you will need**. This means utensils, such as knives, spoons, saucepans and so on, and all the ingredients listed in the recipe.

Get Steady!

Remember, kitchens can be dangerous places, so make sure that you know how to cook safely and carefully.

!
- KNIVES are for CUTTING! Always cut with the knife blade pointed away from you.
- BOILING LIQUIDS can SCALD your skin, and HOT FOOD can BURN! Always turn pan handles away from the front of the cooker.
- ELECTRICITY can give you a SHOCK! Don't let water get anywhere near electric sockets.

Got everything organised?
Now you're all set to

Get Cooking!

Identifying what is clear and appealing

3.3

Read the ten tips below on how to write clearly and in an interesting way.
Some examples have been filled in – make notes listing those that are missing.

How has the writer made the advice clear and easy to understand?	Examples
1. She has introduced the advice and said why it will be useful.	'to make sure that you have a really good time in the kitchen'
2. The advice is divided into sections with headings.	**'Get Ready!'** 'Get Steady!'
3. She uses imperatives to tell her readers what they should do.	
4. She has given explanations of important words.	
5. She uses connectives to organise her ideas and to show links.	'Before you start cooking'
How has she made the advice appealing to young children?	
6. She has chosen words that make the cooking sound fun.	
7. She uses expressive, powerful words.	'shining example'
8. She asks rhetorical questions. These keep the reader interested and involved.	'Are you nearly ready to get cooking?'
9. Exclamation marks are used to make it sound more exciting.	
10. There are visual and taste images. These appeal to the reader's imagination.	'yummy dishes'

3.4 Now read Jamie Oliver's recipe for 'Simple Chocolate Tart'.

Simple **Chocolate Tart**

This chocolate tart is great for those chocofreaks who turn up out of the blue as it is dead quick to make. I think this particular tart cries out for a slightly thicker pastry shell. The better the chocolate you can buy, the tastier it will be.

1 tart shell, baked blind
315 ml/11 fl oz double cream
2 level tablespoons caster sugar
the smallest pinch of salt
115g/4oz butter, softened
455g/1lb best-quality cooking chocolate, broken up
100 ml/3¾ fl oz milk
cocoa powder for dusting

Place the double cream, sugar and pinch of salt in a pan and bring to the boil. As soon as the mixture has boiled, remove from the heat and add the butter and chocolate. Stir until it has completely melted. Allow the mixture to cool slightly, stirring in the cold milk until smooth and shiny. Sometimes this mixture looks like it has split. Allow to cool down a bit more and whisk in a little extra cold milk until smooth. Scrape all the mixture into the cooked and cooled pastry shell with a spatula. Shake the tart to even it out and allow to cool for around 1–2 hours until it is at room temperature. Dust with the cocoa powder. Ultimately the pastry should be short and crisp and the filling should be smooth and should cut like butter.

Find one example of each of these features:

- a word or words that make you think that the tart will taste delicious (expressive words)
- words or phrases that show that he is writing for a teenage or older audience
- imperative verbs (verbs that tell you to do something)
- words that tell the reader exactly when to do something (connectives)
- words that describe how the mixture should look (visual images)
- words that tell you have it should feel (tactile images)
- short, clear sentences.

 The recipe says that it is great for 'chocofreaks'. What do you think this means?

3.5 Write your own favourite recipe in no more than 250 words. It could be for something to eat or to drink. Try to make it appeal to readers of your own age. If you like, it could be for something imaginary – like a 'Valentine's cake'.

Use the same structure as Jamie Oliver:

● title – give it a name that makes it sound good

● short description of the dish – what sort of people might like it, and why

● list of ingredients – use adjectives to make clear exactly the sort of ingredients that are needed

● careful, step-by-step description of what to do – if you like, you could number the steps to make it even clearer

● description of what the dish should look like and how it will taste when it's finished.

3.6 Read through this possible exam question but do not answer it yet.

Write a short advice column about babysitting for a teenage magazine or website.

You might write about:

● the advantages of babysitting as a part-time job

● babysitting and safety

● how to entertain and look after young children.

 Examiner's Tips

In an exam question, use the bullet points to help you to organise your ideas.

Selecting relevant points

3.7

First, copy and complete this brainstorm.
Remember, any ideas, good or bad, can be written down.
You can then select the best ideas and use them to plan your writing.

only babysit for families known or recommended to you

you can earn money without having to get up early

babysitting advice

reading a storybook can be a good way to get children ready for sleep

some children are afraid of the dark, so find out if they have a nightlight

be prepared to be firm about bedtime

your work is not far from home

3.8

Now, start to organise your ideas. Copy the table below, adding the rest of the ideas from the spidergram (including your own) into the correct columns.

Section One Points about what you can get out of babysitting	Section Two Points about safety	Section Three Points about looking after young children
• you can earn money without having to get up early	• only babysit for families known or recommended to you	• be prepared to be firm about bedtime

Writing in paragraphs

Here's how Mehmet, a Year 11 GCSE student, wrote up the points about looking after young children:

Looking after young children can be fun, especially if you've had lots of practice with your own younger relations. However, you do need to be aware of some useful skills. I thought I knew all about it, because I often look after my two-year-old nephew. Even so, the first time I babysat for our neighbours' four-year-old twins was no picnic. I was amazed at just how difficult it can be! By eleven o'clock, my mind was spinning. I was flat out on the sofa, my clothes were covered in toothpaste, and the twins were asleep at least – but in Monsters, Inc sleeping bags, on top of their parents' bed!

Here's what I learned. First, find out what time the children are supposed to go to bed, what their routines are, and stick to them. Don't let them fool you that their other babysitter is much nicer, brings them sweets to eat in bed, and always lets them stay up late. It's not true!

Next, have some ideas ready for quiet activities before bedtime, for instance, reading a picture book. When you've got them into bed, they may want to keep a light on in the bedroom if they are frightened of the dark. Funnily enough, this helps some children to go to sleep more easily. Try not to let them get out of bed again once they're in. Once you've got hold of these basic skills, you're more likely to have a nice, peaceful evening.

3.9

Discuss Mehmet's three paragraphs.

?

Has Mehmet used:

- clear topic sentences?
- helpful connectives?
- sentences of different lengths?
- the present tense?
- imperative verbs?
- a clear, but not too bossy approach?

Mehmet also includes a personal anecdote, when he describes his own babysitting experiences with four-year-old twins. How does this improve the paragraph? Choose one of the statements below and explain why you agree with it.

> "Mehmet shows that boys can be good at looking after young children"

> "His story is quite funny and it makes the reader more interested in him"

> "It's a personal example, so it shows that he knows what he's talking about"

3.10

Finish the advice column.

- Start by copying out the introductory paragraph below.
- Use the points in your table for sections one and two.
- Add your own personal anecdote to section three.
- Finally, add a short conclusion. Write three or four sentences to sum up your advice. Tell your readers why babysitting is a good part-time job, as long as they follow your advice.

Babysitting. It's not all fun and games

Have you ever been asked to babysit for a neighbour or member of your family? Imagine a house or flat full of toddlers, Harry Potter dolls and My Little Ponies. Is this where you'd want to spend Friday night? Probably not! Yet these days, babysitting is a popular way for teenagers to earn extra spending money.

Use the skills developed in this unit to answer this practice question.

Your cousin has been told that her parents have agreed to buy her a mobile phone. Write a letter in which you give advice on how to choose the best and most suitable phone.

You could include advice on:

- where to go/not to go to buy a phone
- the different kinds of phones and functions available
- how to make sure your phone bills don't get too high
- how to look after your mobile phone.

SUMMARY

- Use planning diagrams to get your ideas ordered.
- Use imperative verbs for definite advice/instruction.
- Use confident, relevant points, but don't be too bossy.

POETRY FROM DIFFERENT CULTURES AND TRADITIONS

In the next two units, you will:

- read poems from a variety of cultures and traditions
- read poems that use a dialect and even a different language
- explore a wide range of ideas and feelings about cultures and traditions.

You will learn how to:

- find the story in a poem
- appreciate the use of language and structure in poetry
- explore poetry in more depth
- write about more than one poem.

Where does this fit in the exam?

Paper 2 Section A

How long will I have in the exam?

You will have about 45 minutes to write your response. You will have to choose one of two tasks, and write about two or three poems.

How will this unit help?

You will focus on ten key poems, and study how to compare poems with similar themes.

Culture is a word that means a lot of different things. It refers to everything that makes up the way of life of a particular group of people: language, arts, history, religion, ideas and traditions. One country may contain many different cultures. For instance, some parts of the UK are very multicultural.

Tradition is a part of culture. It refers to beliefs or customs handed down from one generation to the next within a particular culture. These help to give people a cultural identity.

Read through this list of useful terms before you start this section.

accent	the different pronunciation of words or phrases according to where someone comes from, for example 'Unrelated Incidents' uses 'wia' for 'with a'. It is not the same as dialect
dialect	a regional variety of a language, with differences in vocabulary and grammar, for example 'ah rass' in 'Half-caste' is an expression unknown in Standard English
image	a picture in your mind, created by the words of a poem
language	the specific choice of words and phrases in the poem and how they have been used
mother tongue	the first language a child learns at home
Standard English	the form of the English language used in formal situations and often considered 'correct'
stanza	a group of lines from a poem organised together on the page
structure	the way the poem is organised. Includes: stanzas or verses, length of lines, punctuation, and the ordering of the ideas in the poem

About the poets

On these two pages are some brief details about the poets who are featured in this section of the book. It is important that you do not regard these details as giving you the answers to the poems – they are here simply to give you some background to the writers' works. The poems must stand or fall on their own.

There are also some brief comments from students who have read or studied the poems. These show that the poems are not just exam texts, but real texts for you to respond to.

The poets

Tatamkhula Afrika grew up in South Africa. Born in Egypt, he was the son of Arab and Turkish parents. As a member of the African National Congress, he was banned from public speaking and writing. He changed his name so that he could still express his views.

Poem: 'Nothing's Changed'

Grace Nichols grew up in Guyana in the West Indies and came to the UK in 1977. Her first poetry book *I is a Long-Memoried Woman,*was published soon after she came to England.

Poems: 'Island Man', 'Hurricane Hits England'

Lawrence Ferlinghetti was born in New York in 1919. He is known as a 'Beat' poet. The Beats were a group of writers and artists who protested against the American way of life and world politics. He now lives and writes in San Francisco.

Poem: 'Two Scavengers in a Truck, Two Beautiful People in a Mercedes'

Chinua Achebe was born in Nigeria in 1930. He has lived and studied in England and Africa. He believes strongly in African oral traditions. He has said that 'any good story… should have a message, should have a purpose'.

Poem: 'Vultures'

Students' views

This poem made me feel really angry.

I wish my dreams were like the ones in 'Island Man'.
I remember my parents telling me about this hurricane.

Reading this poem is like watching a film!

How can people be so cruel

The poets

Students' views

Denise Levertov was born in England in 1932, but lived her adult life in America. She started writing poetry before she reached her teens, and she went on to become one of America's best-known poets. She died in 1997.

Poem: 'What Were They Like?'

This poem is so sad. I learned about the Vietnam War.

Sujata Bhatt was born in India in 1956. She now lives in Germany. Her first language is Gujarati, and although she writes in English, some of her poems also contain lines in Gujarati. She sees herself as bi-cultural.

Poem: 'Search for my Tongue'

I wish I could speak two languages.

Tom Leonard is a Scottish poet. He is well known for his poetry written using an authentic Glasgow voice. He published his first book in 1969. His poems are highly critical of 'language snobbery'.

Poem: From 'Unrelated Incidents'

I'd like to hear the news using our local dialect.

John Agard was born in Guyana and came to the UK in 1977 with his partner, Grace Nichols. As a child he was interested in the 'sound of words'. He has been a teacher, but now works as a writer and performer of poetry.

Poem: 'Half-Caste'

This poem really made me think about racism.

Moniza Alvi was born in Pakistan, but grew up in Hertfordshire. She worked as a teacher and won her first poetry prize in 1991. Many of her poems are said to be 'surreal'. They contain images from dreams and the imagination.

Poem: 'Presents from my Aunts in Pakistan'

I've got a friend who wears clothes like the ones in this poem.

UNIT 1   POEMS FROM CLUSTER ONE

Nothing's Changed

Small round hard stones click
under my heels,
seeding grasses thrust
bearded seeds
5 into trouser cuffs, cans,
trodden on, crunch
in tall, purple-flowering,
amiable weeds.

District Six.
10 No board says it is:
but my feet know,
and my hands,
and the skin about my bones,
and the soft labouring of my lungs,
15 and the hot, white, inwards turning
anger of my eyes.

Brash with glass,
name flaring like a flag,
it squats
20 in the grass and weeds,
incipient Port Jackson trees:
new, up-market, haute cuisine,
guard at the gatepost,
whites only inn.

25 No sign says it is:
But we know where we belong.

I press my nose
to the clear panes, know,
before I see them, there will be
30 crushed ice white glass,
linen falls,
the single rose.

Down the road,
working man's cafe sells
35 bunny chows.
Take it with you, eat
it at a plastic table's top,
wipe your fingers on your jeans,
spit a little on the floor:
40 it's in the bone.

I back from the glass,
boy again,
leaving small mean O
of small, mean mouth.
45 Hands burn
for a stone, a bomb,
to shiver down the glass.
Nothing's changed.

Tatamkhulu Afrika

amiable: friendly
brash: bright and boastful
Port Jackson trees: trees imported from Port
Jackson, Australia
bunny chows: bread stuffed with pilchards,
often eaten by poor people in South Africa
incipient: starting to grow
haute cuisine: cookery of a very high standard

What story does the poem tell?

The narrator walks through District Six, an area of Cape Town. In the 1960s, this district was declared a 'whites only' area and much of it was destroyed. The poet remembers that time. New buildings are now going up. He comes to a stylish new restaurant with a guard at the gate. Nearby there is a workers' cafe, where the black people go. Although the country's political system has changed, the inequalities between black and white people are still there.

> **?** How does the poet feel at the end of the poem?
> What does he want to do?

Linking images to feelings

.1 Poets use powerful images to convey their feelings. Copy and complete the sentences below. They focus on a description from each stanza which helps to show us how the poet feels. The first has been completed for you.

Stanza One
'in tall, purple-flowering, amiable weeds.'
The district is overgrown, but friendly.

Stanza Two
'the hot, white, inwards turning anger of my eyes'
His memories of District Six make him feel...

Stanza Three
'Brash with glass, name flaring like a flag'
The new restaurant seems...

Stanza Four
'No sign says it is:
But we know where we belong.'
The signs have gone, but he still feels that he is not... in the classy restaurant.

Stanza Five
'crushed ice white glass,
linen falls,
the single rose'
Everything in the new restaurant is...

Stanza Six
'wipe your fingers on your jeans,
spit a little on the floor:'
He feels angry and shamed because the cafe where the black people can go is so...

Stanza Seven
'boy again...
Hands burn
for a stone...'
He wants to destroy the new restaurant because he feels... and...

Using short lines and sentences

Writers use all sorts of ways to tell their stories. Sometimes the choice of one word rather than another can change the story. On other occasions the use of punctuation or line length can say a great deal. Think about the difference between:

Whites only
and
Will people of alternative colour please refrain from entering the building

The message is the same, but the way it is delivered is very different.

Most of the sentences in this poem are long, but the lines are short. In fact, some of the stanzas could be said not to be in 'real' sentences. However, they do give detailed descriptions of the place and tell us about the poet's feelings.

Then, at two key moments in the poem, there are short, complete sentences. These are in lines 25–6, and 48 (the last line).

Look at them now. They draw our attention to important facts or ideas in the poem.

1.2 **Write a sentence to explain each of these ideas in your own words. You can use longer sentences to explain what they mean, or what the poet is feeling.**

 Why do you think they have been placed halfway through the poem and at the end?

Using contrasts

As you will see in other poems in this book, writers often contrast two sets of people, ideas, places or experiences. Sometimes the writer doesn't announce it to the reader, but just places them alongside each other. This is called 'juxtaposition'.

1.3 **Look at the contrasts and juxtaposition in this poem.**

 What does the 'hot anger' (lines 15 and 16) and the 'burn' of the hands (line 45) contrast with? Look at the fifth stanza.

 What two places are compared?

Reading closely

As you have discovered from your reading, a key point in the poem is when the poet realises that though the outward rules of apartheid have gone, he still cannot get the things that rich, white people have.

'No sign says it is:
But we know where we belong.'

.4 **These questions below are difficult, but discuss them with a partner and see if you can arrive at some answers.**

- Why do you think the poet says his feet 'know' where they are, and know it is District Six?

- Why does he mention the imported 'Port Jackson' trees? Is this saying something about the people who have built the posh restaurant?

- Why does the poet say 'It's in the bone' when he talks about wiping his fingers on his jeans, spitting on the floor? Is he saying that he and the other working men *deserve* to be in the poor cafe?

- Finally, why does he say he is a 'boy again', when he presses against the window of the restaurant?

Discovering more

'Nothing's Changed' is set in Cape Town in South Africa. People of many different races live there. The government wanted to keep all the country's wealth and power for white people. They brought in *apartheid*, a system based on the idea of 'separate development' of black and white people.

.5 **Use the library or the Internet to find out more about apartheid.**

- When did apartheid officially end in South Africa?

- What was the name of the political party that gained power when white rule was ended?

- Who was its leader?

Island Man

(for a Caribbean island man in London who still wakes
up to the sound of the sea)

Morning
and island man wakes up
to the sound of blue surf
in his head
5   the steady breaking and wombing

wild seabirds
and fishermen pushing out to sea
the sun surfacing defiantly
from the east
10   of his small emerald island
he always comes back   groggily groggily

Comes back to sands
of a grey metallic soar

                                          to surge of wheels

15   to dull North Circular roar

muffling muffling
his crumpled pillow waves
island man heaves himself

Another London day

Grace Nichols

> **defiantly:** challengingly
> **groggily:** feeling weak or dizzy,
> as if he had drunk too much alcohol
> **North Circular:** a very busy road
> around North London

What is the story of the poem?

Grace Nichols describes a man from a Caribbean island
waking up in England. His head is still full of dreams of his
beautiful island. These contrast strongly with the grey city
morning he encounters as he wakes to 'another London day'.

 Do you think the man has
recently arrived in
England, or has he been
here for some while?

Using sights and sounds

Poets often appeal to our senses of sight and sound in verse.
This is especially true of Grace Nichols' poem.

.6

Copy and complete the diagram below. Fill in more of the sights he sees and sounds he hears in his dream and in London.

In the dream island, he sees:	In London, he sees:
1. wild seabirds	1. a grey metallic soar
2. _____	2. his crumpled pillow
3. _____	

... and he hears:	... and he hears:
1. the sound of blue surf	1. _____
2. _____	2. _____

The images and sounds which the poet has described help us to see the differences between the two places. Write two or three sentences, explaining in your own words why you think the Island Man still dreams of his island.

Using rhyme and repetition

Grace Nichols has used rhymes and repeated words and sounds to draw attention to the man's feelings.

.7

Discuss and then write down your own answers to these questions.

?
- How many 'ing' words can you find?
- What does the repetition of these words suggest? (Think of the sea.)
- What other words and phrases are repeated?
- What ideas and feelings about waking in London do these words emphasise?

Reading closely

.8

Why is the word 'island' so important in this poem?

Write down all the possible connections it can have with the poem. Use these to help you get started:

England is part of an island, so...
If you are on an island you might feel...

Two Scavengers in a Truck, Two Beautiful People in a Mercedes

　　　　At the stoplight waiting for the light
　　　　　　　　　　nine a.m. downtown San Francisco
　　　a bright yellow garbage truck
　　　　　　　with two garbagemen in red plastic blazers
5　　　standing on the back stoop
　　　　　　　　　one on each side hanging on
　　　and looking down into
　　　　　　　　　an elegant open Mercedes
　　　　　with an elegant couple in it
10　The man
　　　　　　in a hip three-piece linen suit
　　　　　　　　with shoulder-length blond hair & sunglasses
　　　The young blond woman so casually coifed
　　　　　　　　with a short skirt and colored stockings
15　　　on the way to his architect's office

　　　And the two scavengers up since four a.m.
　　　　　　　　　　grungy from their route
　　　　　　　on the way home
　　　The older of the two with grey iron hair
20　　　　　　　　　　and hunched back
　　　　　looking down like some
　　　　　　　　　gargoyle Quasimodo
　　　And the younger of the two
　　　　　　　　also with sunglasses & long hair
25　　　about the same age as the Mercedes driver

　　　And both scavengers gazing down
　　　　　　　　　　as from a great distance
　　　　　　　at the cool couple
　　　as if they were watching some odorless TV ad
30　　　　　　in which everything is always possible

　　　And the very red light for an instant
　　　　　　　　holding all four close together
　　　　　as if anything at all were possible
　　　　　　　　　　between them
35　　　across that small gulf
　　　　　　　in the high seas
　　　　　　　　　of this democracy

Lawrence Ferlinghetti

> **garbage truck:** rubbish lorry
> **stoop:** step
> **elegant:** stylish and graceful
> **blazers:** jackets
> **casually coifed:** with a casual hairstyle
> **grungy:** dirty and scruffy
> **gargoyle:** a hideously ugly carved head
> **scavengers:** creatures that feed on dead flesh
> **odorless:** having no smell

Discovering more

1.9

What do you know about the story of Quasimodo?

You may have seen the film *The Hunchback of Notre-Dame*.
Find out what happens to him, and how he is treated by the people of Paris.

What is the story of the poem?

The poem is set on a busy road in San Francisco, USA. Two 'garbagemen', hanging on to the back of a truck, look down and see a rich young couple in an open-topped car. The poet shows how different these two pairs of people are. Yet for a moment, they are alongside each other, level.

 .10 Discuss these two questions.

> **?** Why do you think the poet brings them together for a moment at the traffic lights?

> **?** Do they share any of the same hopes or dreams?

Comparing the characters

Many poems work by contrasting two people or sets of experiences (see 'Island Man' for example).

 .11 Copy and complete the table below. To do so, find eight quotations from the poem to show the differences between the 'two scavengers' and the 'elegant couple'.

The Two Scavengers	The Elegant Couple
'in red plastic blazers'	'The man/ in a hip three-piece linen suit'

Now, explain what each of your selected quotations tells you about the characters. For example,

The two scavengers are wearing 'red plastic blazers'. They are brightly coloured to make the men visible while they are working on busy streets, but they are not stylish.

Now reread lines 16–37 of the poem. Explain what you think the garbagemen might be thinking as they look down at the couple in the Mercedes. Think carefully about the reference to the 'TV ad'.

> **?** Why do you think the poet compares the older man with Quasimodo?

Using layout

.12 This poem has an unusual layout. Pick the two explanations from the box that you agree with most strongly. For each one, write one or two more sentences, saying why you agree.

- It is to make it look 'free', because America is supposed to be 'the land of the free'.
- It makes the reader's eye move back and forth, as if you are looking from the Mercedes to the garbage truck.
- It makes the poem look restless, like the busy San Francisco traffic.

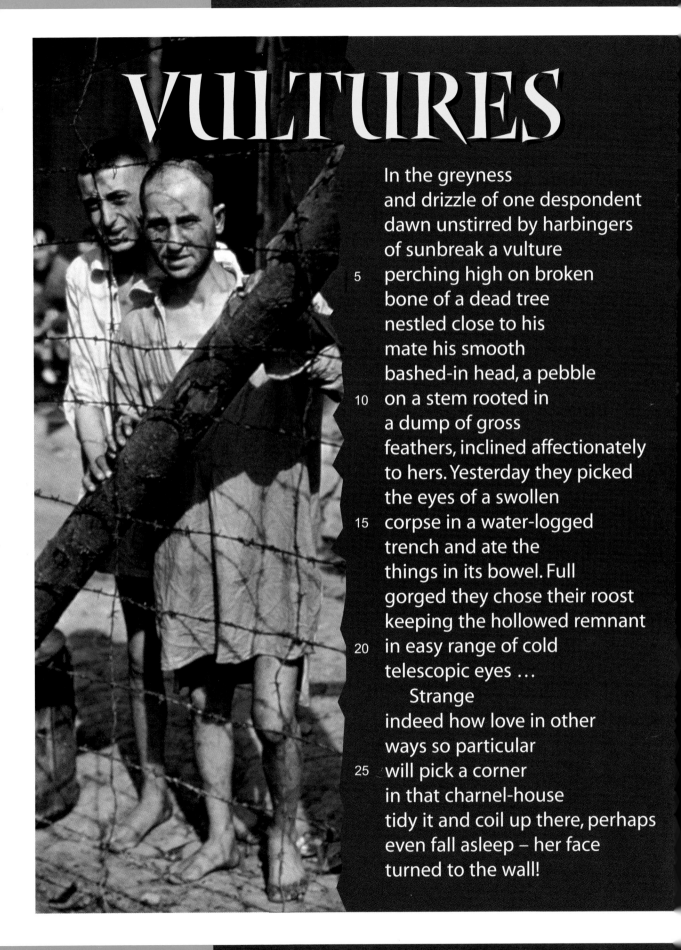

VULTURES

In the greyness
and drizzle of one despondent
dawn unstirred by harbingers
of sunbreak a vulture
5　perching high on broken
bone of a dead tree
nestled close to his
mate his smooth
bashed-in head, a pebble
10　on a stem rooted in
a dump of gross
feathers, inclined affectionately
to hers. Yesterday they picked
the eyes of a swollen
15　corpse in a water-logged
trench and ate the
things in its bowel. Full
gorged they chose their roost
keeping the hollowed remnant
20　in easy range of cold
telescopic eyes ...
　　Strange
indeed how love in other
ways so particular
25　will pick a corner
in that charnel-house
tidy it and coil up there, perhaps
even fall asleep – her face
turned to the wall!

30 ...Thus the Commandant at Belsen
Camp going home for
the day with fumes of
human roast clinging
rebelliously to his hairy
35 nostrils will stop
at the wayside sweet-shop
and pick up a chocolate
for his tender offspring
waiting at home for Daddy's
40 return...
    Praise bounteous
providence if you will
that grants even an ogre
a tiny glow-worm
45 tenderness encapsulated
in icy caverns of a cruel
heart or else despair
for in the very germ
of that kindred love is
50 lodged the perpetuity
of evil.

Chinua Achebe

harbingers: messengers who
announce an arrival
charnel-house: house where
dead bodies or bones are
placed
the Commandant at Belsen:
the officer in charge of a
World War Two Nazi
concentration camp
bounteous providence: the
generosity of God
despondent: sad
encapsulated: summed up
kindred: related
perpetuity: unchanging state

What is the story of the poem?

'Vultures' is a poem that raises difficult questions.

In it, Chinua Achebe describes the behaviour of carrion-eaters – birds that eat other dead creatures in order to feed their 'loved ones'– at a Nazi concentration camp in World War Two. The second part of the poem describes the man who runs the camp going home to his children, the smell of death still in his nostrils.

It will help if you know a little about what happened in the Holocaust (the time when many millions of people were kept in camps by the Nazis and then killed).

1.13 Speak to your English teacher, or your History teacher, about the conditions in these concentration camps.

Getting inside the poem

1.14 Look at the overall picture and atmosphere of the poem. Skim through the poem and select words that stand out. You might start with:

| greyness | bone | drizzle | corpse |

Write down your first impressions in a sentence or two. Is the tone:

| bright? | hopeful? | dark? | sombre? | horrifying? |

? Are there surprising words or images that *don't* seem to fit the general tone?

Here is one student's first impressions.

The poem feels lifeless, because of the 'bones' and 'corpses'... and it all takes place in a 'charnel house', a place where dead bodies are placed. This poem seems like a vision of hell.

? Do you agree?

? What could you add?

Exploring structure

15 The poem has been divided below into five sections (A–E).
For each statement below, make a note of the lines it describes.
The first has been done for you.

Then write down one or two questions raised in your mind by each section of the poem.

	Statement	Lines	Question
A	The poet describes two vultures, sitting in a dead tree. They behave affectionately towards each other.	Lines 1–13	*How can such ugly birds love each other?*
B	He explains that yesterday they ate a dead creature.		
C	He says what he thinks about their behaviour.		
D	He compares the vultures to a Nazi Commandant, who has prisoners killed, but also loves his own children.		
E	He gives his readers a choice of reactions to this mixture of love and hatred.	Lines 41–51	

Using images and descriptions

Chinua Achebe has used powerful images and descriptions to express his ideas. Some of these are metaphors, others straight descriptions.

16 Discuss the following questions.

- Why does he use the metaphor, 'a broken bone of a dead tree' to describe a broken branch? Think about where the poem is set.
- What does the phrase 'human roast' refer to?
- Why is 'tenderness' described as being like a 'tiny glow-worm'?

Giving the reader a choice

Poets often create a dialogue with their readers, raising questions for them to consider. Look again at the choice offered at the end of the poem.

17 Overall, does the poem make you feel hope or despair?
Write about 75 words explaining your choice.

What Were They Like?

1) Did the people of Viet Nam
   use lanterns of stone?
2) Did they hold ceremonies
   to reverence the opening of buds?
3) Were they inclined to quiet laughter?
4) Did they use bone and ivory,
   jade and silver, for ornament?
5) Had they an epic poem?
6) Did they distinguish between speech and singing?

1) Sir, their light hearts turned to stone.
   It is not remembered whether in gardens
   stone lanterns illumined pleasant ways.
2) Perhaps they gathered once to delight in blossom,
   but after the children were killed
   there were no more buds.
3) Sir, laughter is bitter to the burned mouth.
4) A dream ago, perhaps. Ornament is for joy.
   All the bones were charred.
5) It is not remembered. Remember,
   most were peasants; their life
   was in rice and bamboo.
   When peaceful clouds were reflected in the paddies
   and the water buffalo stepped surely along terraces,
   maybe fathers told their sons old tales.
   When bombs smashed those mirrors
   there was time only to scream.
6) There is an echo yet
   of their speech which was like a song.
   It was reported their singing resembled
   the flight of moths in moonlight.
   Who can say? It is silent now.

Denise Levertov

reverence: praise
jade: a semi-precious stone, usually green
epic poem: a long poem about the deeds of heroes in myth or history
distinguish: know the difference
illumined: lit up
paddies: water-filled rice fields
resembled: was like

Getting inside the poem

1.18

Use the library or the Internet to find out more about the Vietnam war and present your findings to the class or a small group.

Who was it between?
Why did it start?
When did it end?
What were its effects?

What is the story of the poem?

The question-and-answer structure of this poem describes the devastation caused by the Vietnam War. The first stanza asks questions about life before the war. The second stanza provides the answers.

Using questions and answers

19 Copy and complete the table below. For each change that took place, write down one word or phrase that shows how beautiful the country was before the war.

Before the war	After the war
'their light hearts' 'they gathered once to delight in blossom'	'turned to stone' 'there were no more buds' 'burned mouth' 'the bones were charred' 'silent now'

Reading closely

The poet's questions are hard to answer. They show how much of a country's culture can be lost when there is a war. For example, answer number 1 says that, 'It is not remembered'.
In the very last line, the narrator says,
'Who can say? It is silent now.'

20 Find four more words or phrases that show loss or forgetting.

Showing rather than telling

Much good writing is about showing rather than telling. This poem would not be effective if it just said, 'War is bad and destroys people's lives and culture'.

21 What else does this poem show us, as well as telling us how bad war is?

You could start:

It shows us the lives of Vietnamese people, and gives us a picture of...

Writing about more than one poem

The next four pages look at the skills required when you are asked to compare two or more poems. Essentially, this means writing about similarities and differences between them.

Here you will be looking at two different ways in which you can approach your exam essay.

Approach 1:
The first way follows a simple process:

● Write about one poem.
● Write about the second poem.
● Discuss similarities and differences in the key area from the question.
● Sum up your ideas.

You will have about 15–20 minutes to write on each poem, so it is a good idea to get writing straight away. Do your planning before the exam.

Make sure in your essay that for each poem you:

● support each point you make with at least one quotation
● refer at least once to a language effect (such as the use of contrasts) and its effect.

1.22

Now look at the following title:

> **Compare the ways in which the poets present people's feelings about different places in 'Island Man' and one other poem from Cluster One.**

Here is the first paragraph from an answer.

'Island Man' is about a man waking up in London still dreaming about his old life in the Caribbean. He hears the traffic and, because he is dozing, thinks it sounds like the waves for a moment. He wishes he wasn't in London.

 Does this paragraph do everything it should?

.23 **Now look at this version.**

'Island Man' is about a man waking up in London 'to the sound of blue surf', still dreaming about his old life in the Caribbean. He hears the traffic and, because he is dozing, thinks it sounds like the waves for a moment. He wishes he wasn't in London, calling it 'dull' and just 'another... day'.

 How is this better?

 Can you think of any special language effects that could have been mentioned as well?

.24 **Choose one other poem from those you have looked at, and write a first paragraph similar to the one above.**

- Describe what happens in the poem.
- Use a suitable quotation (line or words from the poem).
- Mention a language effect (for example, rhyme, simile etc).

> **Approach 2:**
> This is more difficult.
> It compares the two poems *together*, looking at key areas from the title.

This plan is for the same question. It is comparing 'Island Man' with 'Nothing's Changed'.

Paragraph 1: **Introduction**	Quick recap on both poems. How are they similar and different? Both have strong feelings. Different settings. But both people isolated – on islands?
Paragraph 2: **Places and feelings**	'Island Man': London and Caribbean island. Misses his home/culture. 'Nothing's Changed': Anger because Cape Town still segregated after end of apartheid.
Paragraph 3: **Language**	'Island Man': Contrasting language – London and Caribbean island. Sight and sound images. Rhymes. Repetitions to show dull routine in London, and sound of waves, traffic. 'Nothing's Changed': Contrasts between restaurants for rich/poor people.
Paragraph 4: **Structure**	'Island Man': Two halves. First deals with Caribbean, second London. 'Nothing's Changed': Two halves. Shorter sentence in middle. Shows divisions.
Paragraph 5: **Conclusion**	How I feel about the poems.

Here, a student called Sally has attempted the first two paragraphs, based on the plan you have just read:

'Island Man' by Grace Nichols and 'Nothing's Changed' by Tatamkhula Afrika are both about people who feel strongly about the places in their lives. 'Island Man' is about a man who has come from a Caribbean island to live in London. In 'Nothing's Changed', the poet describes how he feels about a district of Cape Town, South Africa, where he used to live. Both are isolated on 'islands' of different sorts.

In 'Island Man', Grace Nichols shows how different life is in London and the Caribbean. The island man feels homesick when he remembers his beloved 'small emerald island'. He has to get up and deal with 'another London day'. On the other hand, in 'Nothing's Changed', the poet returns to his old home. He feels angry because his country is now supposed to treat black and white people equally, but in reality 'nothing's changed'.

1.25 Help Sally to develop the essay.

Look at paragraphs 3 and 4 in Sally's essay plan on page 87.

First, jot down one or two quotations from each poem to back up each of the points she plans to make.

 Examiner's Tips

A good way to show that you can back up your ideas is to try to fit short quotations from the poems into your sentences. Look at the examples in the second paragraph of Sally's essay.

1.26 Now write paragraphs 3 and 4.

Use this first sentence to help you begin:

Grace Nichols uses beautiful sight and sound images to show the island man's love for his island. For example...

.27 Now write your own comparison.

Compare the presentation of cruelty towards people of different cultures in 'Vultures' and 'What Were They Like?'.

If you choose Approach 1:
● Write about one poem.
● Write about the second poem.
● Discuss similarities and differences in the key area from the question.
● Sum up your ideas.

If you choose Approach 2:
Write about key areas as you go along.

You can use this table to help you.

Section of essay	Possible sentence starters
1. Introduction Introduce the different cultures and explain who in each poem is showing cruelty.	'Vultures' and 'What Were They Like?' both show how cruel human beings can be…
2. Events and feelings Explain what happens in each poem – the basic story (2–3 sentences) and how each poem made you feel (2–3 sentences)	In 'Vultures', two birds are sitting… 'What Were They Like?' has two speakers…
3. Language Find 1–2 examples of powerful language in each poem. Quote each example and then explain how it strengthens the ideas and feelings in the poem (2–3 sentences for each poem).	'Vultures' has powerful images of kindness and of cruelty. For instance… In 'What Were They Like?' descriptions are also used to make a contrast. The poet describes…
4. Structure Describe how each poet has used layout or structure to get his/her ideas across. Compare or contrast between the poems.	The layout in 'What Were They Like?' is based on questions. This helps the poem work because…
5. Conclusion Sum up by writing what you think each poem is saying about cruelty between different cultures. Give your own opinion.	In conclusion, it is clear that 'What Were They Like?' is very sympathetic to…

UNIT 2　POEMS FROM CLUSTER TWO

From Search For My Tongue

You ask me what I mean
by saying I have lost my tongue.
I ask you, what would you do
if you had two tongues in your mouth,
5　and lost the first one, the mother tongue,
and could not really know the other,
the foreign tongue.
You could not use them both together
even if you thought that way.
10　And if you lived in a place you had to
speak a foreign tongue,
your mother tongue would rot,
rot and die in your mouth
until you had to spit it out.
15　I thought I spit it out
but overnight while I dream,

મને હતું કે આખ્ખી જીભ આખ્ખી ભાષા,
(munay hutoo kay aakhee jeebh aakhee bhasha)

મેં થૂંકી નાખી છે.
20　(may thoonky nakhi chay)

પરંતુ રાત્રે સપનામાં મારી ભાષા પાછી આવે છે.
(parantoo rattray svupnama mari bhasha pachi aavay chay)

ફૂલની જેમ મારી ભાષા મારી જીભ
(foolnee jaim mari bhasha nmari jeebh)

25　મોઢામાં ખીલે છે.
(modhama kheelay chay)

ફૂલની જેમ મારી ભાષા મારી જીભ
(fullnee jaim mari bhasha mari jeebh)

મોઢામાં પાકે છે.
30　(modhama pakay chay)

it grows back, a stump of a shoot
grows longer, grows moist, grows strong ve[i]
it ties the other tongue in knots,
the bud opens, the bud opens in my mouth,
35　it pushes the other tongue aside.
Everytime I think I've forgotten,
I think I've lost the mother tongue,
it blossoms out of my mouth.

Sujata Bhatt

Mother tongue: this is the first
language someone learns to speak.
The word 'tongue' means 'language'
Gujarati: one of the main Indian
languages

What is the story of the poem?

The poet is writing about the languages she speaks. Her first language, Gujarati, is her mother tongue. Her second language, English, she describes as a foreign tongue. She describes the 'battle' between the two tongues, or languages, in her mouth.

Exploring the poem

In lines 5–14 the poet describes how she has lost her mother tongue. Complete the bullet points to explain how this has happened.

- Lines 8–9: *it is impossible to use two languages at the same time*

- Lines 10–12: ....

- Lines 13–14: ....

In lines 31–38 the poet describes her mother tongue growing back. She uses the image of a plant to illustrate this.

From the poem, make a list of all the words you associate with a growing plant.

> **?** Why do you think the poet uses the metaphor of a plant to describe her tongue, or language?

Looking at structure and language

The middle of the poem (lines 17–30) is written in Gujarati. These lines have the same meaning as the English lines which follow. Each line of Gujarati script is followed by a version that enables readers of English to pronounce it.

Have a go at reading the Gujarati words.

Before and after the Gujarati words the poet says:

'I thought I spit it out
but overnight while I dream
it grows back…'

> **?**
> - Why do you think it 'grows back' while she dreams?
> - The poem is called 'Search For My Tongue'. Which language does the poet feel most comfortable with?
> - How does the poet feel about having two languages?

> **?** We are not used to seeing language we do not understand on the page. If Gujarati is not your mother tongue, how do you feel seeing it on the page next to English? Does it give you some understanding of the poet's position?

From Unrelated Incidents

What is the poem about?

Here, the BBC six o'clock news is read in a strong, Scottish accent, probably Glaswegian. It has been written 'phonetically' and describes the speaker's feelings about the issue of 'correct BBC English'.

Understanding the words

Accented word	Standard English version
thi	the
wia	
iz	
coz	
yi	
widny	
wahnt	

2.3

Copy the table above, adding the Standard English version from the choice below.

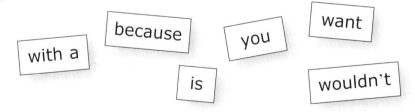

because   you   want

with a   is   wouldn't

Now, complete the table, adding the accented words from lines 10–38 of the poem, and their Standard English versions.

this is thi
six a clock
news thi
man said n
5 thi reason
a talk wia
BBC accent
iz coz yi
widny wahnt
10 mi ti talk
aboot thi
trooth wia
voice lik
wanna yoo
15 scruff. if
a toktaboot
thi trooth
lik wanna yoo
scruff yi
20 widny thingk
it wuz troo.
jist wanna yoo
scruff tokn.
thirza right
25 way ti spell
ana right way
ti tok it. this
is me tokn yir
right way a
30 spellin. this
is ma trooth.
yooz doant no
thi trooth
yirsellz cawz
35 yi canny talk
right. this is
the six a clock
nyooz. belt up.

Tom Leonard

Understanding the message

The six o'clock news is usually read using Standard English pronunciation and dialect. In this poem the poet tells us why he thinks this is.

- The news cannot be read in a 'scruffy' voice.
- If the news is read in a 'scruffy' voice it won't be believed.
- There is a 'right way' to talk.
- There is a 'right way' to spell.

Discuss these four points with a partner and say whether you agree or disagree and why. More importantly, does the poet or speaker agree with them?

In writing this poem the poet is showing that Standard English is not the only way to speak in this country. He seems to be suggesting that people's dialects or accents should be used more in the media. Is he right that they are not used?

- With a partner think of five examples of where spoken dialect or strong accents *are* used on television and in what cases (is it only in drama, comedy etc?)

Looking at structure

Why is so little punctuation used in the poem?

**Add full stops or other punctuation to the poem.
Read the new version of the poem aloud.**

> **?** What is the effect of the punctuated version, and the original?
> Is one version more effective than the other?

Have a look at the last sentence in the final line. It is only two words in length. Why is it so short? Which of these reasons do you most agree with? Write down your own reason, if you prefer.

- He couldn't fit any more words on the line.
- The newsreader is irritated at explaining his ideas.
- It is the last thing you expect a newsreader to say.
- Everyone can understand the words 'belt up'.

Making a statement

One of the most interesting things about this poem is that although it sounds like a newsreader's announcement, what it says is not what would be said on the news.

Make a statement about something you believe in.

Copy the style of Tom Leonard's poem – using your own local dialect and writing phonetically.

Half-Caste

Excuse me
standing on one leg
I'm half-caste

Explain yuself
5   wha yu mean
when yu say half-caste
yu mean when picasso
mix red an green
is a half-caste canvas/
10 explain yuself
wha yu mean
when yu say half-caste
yu mean when light an shadow
mix in de sky
15 is a half-caste weather/
well in dat case
england weather
nearly always half-caste
in fact some o dem cloud
20 half-caste till dem overcast
so spiteful dem dont want de sun pass
ah rass/
explain yuself
wha yu mean
25 when yu say half-caste
yu mean tchaikovsky
sit down at dah piano
an mix a black key
wid a white key
30 is a half-caste symphony/

Explain yuself
wha yu mean
Ah listening to yu wid de keen
half of mih ear
35 Ah lookin at yu wid de keen
half of mih eye
and when I'm introduced to yu
I'm sure you'll understand
why I offer yu half-a-hand
40 an when I sleep at night
I close half-a-eye
consequently when I dream
I dream half-a-dream
an when moon begin to glow
45 I half-caste human being
cast half-a-shadow
but yu must come back tomorrow
wid de whole of yu eye
an de whole of yu ear
50 an de whole of yu mind

an I will tell yu
de other half
of my story

John Agard

half-caste: a term used to describe someone who is born to parents of different colours. The term is now considered to be an insult.
ah rass: this is an expression which shows disgust; it could also be viewed as cursing.

What is the story of the poem?

The speaker is talking to an 'imaginary' person – perhaps the reader of the poem. He imagines this person is someone who uses the term half-caste. Through the poem he shows that the term does not mean half of something but a mixture of two things. The speaker has a particular colour of skin because his parents had different skin colours.

Understanding the poem

.7

Read lines 4–30 to see what the poet is saying about 'half-caste'.
Copy and complete the table.

Idea from poem	What it says about 'half-caste'
'picasso mix red an green'	Picasso was a great painter; he made something beautiful and striking from two colours.
'light an shadow mix in de sky'	
'tchaikovsky sit down at dah piano an mix a black key wid a white key'	

Read lines 32–50. Here the poet develops his view of the term 'half-caste'. He does this by writing about ordinary things that people do and the parts of the body that are used. Copy and complete the table, adding the part of the half-caste body that is used for each action.

Action	Part of the 'half-caste' body
'listening to yu'	'half of mih ear'
'lookin at yu'	
'introduced to yu'	
'sleep at night'	

Which lines say that:

?
- we are not 'whole' people if we see half-caste people as inferior?
- a 'half-caste' person is a 'whole' person?

.8

A Caribbean dialect and accent is used in the poem. Make sure you are clear about the meaning of the words by copying and completing the table below.

Caribbean accent/dialect	Standard English
yuself	yourself

Now, read the poem aloud, perhaps with a partner.

 Should it be read with aggression and punch, or with softness and thoughtfulness – or a mixture of both?

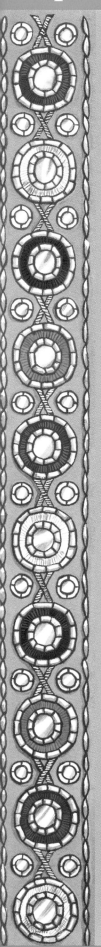

Presents from my Aunts in Pakistan

They sent me a salwar kameez
     peacock-blue,
          and another
   glistening like an orange split open,
5 embossed slippers gold and black
        points curling.
     Candy-striped glass bangles
        snapped, drew blood.
     Like at school, fashions changed
10   in Pakistan –
the salwar bottoms were broad and stiff,
       then narrow.
My aunts chose an apple-green sari,
     silver-bordered
15   for my teens.

I tried each satin-silken top –
     was alien in the sitting-room.
I could never be as lovely
        as those clothes –
20   I longed
for denim and corduroy.
     My costume clung to me
       and I was aflame.
I couldn't rise up out of its fire,
25   half-English,
       unlike Aunt Jamila.

I wanted my parents' camel-skin lamp –
     switching it on in my bedroom,
to consider the cruelty
30   and the transformation
from camel to shade,
     marvel at the colours
       like stained glass.

My mother cherished her jewellery –
35   Indian gold, dangling, filigree,
        But it was stolen from our ca
The presents were radiant in my wardrobe.
     My aunts requested cardigans
       from Marks and Spencers.

40 My salwar kameez
     didn't impress the schoolfriend
who sat on my bed, asked to see
     my weekend clothes.
But often I admired the mirror-work,
45   tried to glimpse myself
       in the miniature
glass circles, recall the story
     how the three of us
       sailed to England.
50 Prickly heat had me screaming on the way.
     I ended up in a cot
in my English grandmother's dining-room,
     found myself alone,
        playing with a tin boat.

55 I pictured my birthplace
     from fifties' photographs.
       When I was older
there was conflict, a fractured land
     throbbing through newsprint.
60 Sometimes I saw Lahore –
     my aunts in shaded rooms,
screened from male visitors,
     sorting presents,
       wrapping them in tissue.

65 Or there were beggars, sweeper-girls
     and I was there –
       of no fixed nationality,
staring through fretwork
     at the Shalimar Gardens.

Moniza Alv

---

salwar: the loose trousers often worn in Pakistan and Bangladesh
kameez: the loose shirt worn over the top of the salwar trousers
sari: the traditional dress worn by women in India and parts of Pakistan
embossed: raised pattern
filigree: a very delicate twisting of materials
mirror work: small mirror circles put on the clothes for decoration
Shalimar Gardens: beautiful gardens in Lahore

What is the story of the poem?

 This question could be answered: 'a girl looks at the clothes her aunts have sent her'? But is that all the story?

..9 **The table below gives a summary of the story of the poem. Find quotations to fit the story stages, and then copy and complete the table.**

She receives presents from her Aunts	They sent me a salwar kameez
She thinks about the English/Western clothes she would like to wear	
She tries on the clothes and likes how they look despite her friend's lack of interest	
She remembers leaving Pakistan with her parents to live in England	
She feels unable to belong totally to either country	

Keep this table safe; you will need it later.

Using colour

The poem does not just tell a simple story, it also creates strong images and appeals to our senses. The colours and items are described in such a way that we can see them in our heads, or almost touch and feel them.

.10 **Make a list of all the different colours that are mentioned in the poem; look particularly at lines 1–40. What items are these colours describing? For example:**

'They sent me a salwar kameez
                    peacock-blue'

Picturing the scene

Like a film, the poet seems to cut from one scene to another. So, one moment she is with a friend in her room, then on a ship, then in a cot in her grandmother's house. Towards the end of the poem she is in Pakistan watching the people and places around her.

 What four groups of people does she picture in her mind? (see lines 60–65)

.11 **Finally, taking your story of the poem, and the work on images, write down an explanation of what this poem is about, supported by examples and quotations.**

Hurricane Hits England

It took a hurricane, to bring her closer
To the landscape.
Half the night she lay awake,
The howling ship of the wind,
5   Its gathering rage,
Like some dark ancestral spectre.
Fearful and reassuring.

Talk to me Huracan
Talk to me Oya
10   Talk to me Shango
And Hattie,
My sweeping, back-home cousin.

Tell me why you visit
An English coast?
15   What is the meaning
Of old tongues
Reaping havoc
In new places?

The blinding illumination,
20   Even as you short-
Circuit us
Into further darkness?

What is the meaning of trees
Falling heavy as whales
25   Their crusted roots
Their cratered graves?

O why is my heart unchained?

Tropical Oya of the Weather,
I am aligning myself to you,
30   I am following the movement of your winds,
I am riding the mystery of your storm.

Ah, sweet mystery,
Come to break the frozen lake in me,
Shaking the foundations of the very trees within me,
35   Come to let me know
That the earth is the earth is the earth.

Grace Nichols

huracan: a word meaning hurricane
Oya: the goddess of wind for the Yoruba people of West Africa
Shango: the god of thunder and lightning for the Yoruba people
Hattie: the name of a famous hurricane that hit the Caribbean

What is the story of the poem?

On the surface, this may seem a very simple tale; the poet lies in bed and a hurricane blows outside. But this tells only half the story.

Understanding the poem

.12 To understand the poem, we need to look at what the poet does and says, but also what she thinks and feels

With a partner, choose a word to describe how the poet feels as she:

- 'lies awake'
- speaks to the hurricane, asks it questions
- talks about her heart being 'unchained'
- 'aligns' herself to the hurricane
- 'follows its movements'
- describes the arrival of the hurricane as a 'sweet mystery'.

You may want to use some of these words:

puzzled   connected   freed

curious   emotional   tired

attracted   happy   understanding

frightened   confused

Using personification

By talking to the hurricane, the poet is treating it as if it were a person or creature. This is called personification.

.13 Reread the poem and write down five words or phrases that personify the hurricane. For example, 'you visit...'.

 Which words make the hurricane seem frightening, exciting or powerful?

Why does the poet call the hurricane 'sweet' at the end?

- The woman lies awake listening to the hurricane.
- The trees are all falling down.
- She decides to give in to the hurricane.
- She asks the hurricane to speak to her.
- She wonders why it is visiting England.
- The hurricane causes a power failure, but the poet understands.
- The woman realises she lives on just one earth.

Looking at structure

.14 Finally, to ensure you are clear about the poem's story, reread it and put the points from the box in the order they occur in the poem.

Writing about more than one poem

At the end of Unit 1, you looked at how a student called Sally planned a comparative essay. You then helped her to complete her essay, following her plan.

2.15 Here is a new task related to two poems from Unit 2.

> **Compare the way the poets feel about belonging to two different cultures in 'Presents from my Aunts in Pakistan' and 'Hurricane Hits England'.**

This time, start by taking the title apart.
You will not be getting so much help this time.

- What are the key words from the title?
- Copy and complete the table.

Key word	Means?
Compare	Write about similarities and differencs

Now, go back to the two poems and read them through again carefully, keeping the question and the key words in mind.

You will be looking for:
- similarities
- differences
- culture
- belonging (to a culture)
- useful quotations (jot them down as you go along).

 Examiner's Tips

It is always a good idea to start simply by stating the 'story' of the poem.

.16 Following a plan

Complete the tasks under each heading to make a written response to the essay title. This plan is just one way of tackling the title. If you have a better way – perhaps by comparing and contrasting as you go along – then use it instead.

Introduction

Write a short, simple explanation of the 'story' of each poem.
For example:

These two poems describe how the poets who are from different countries feel about living in England. The poets come from Pakistan and the Caribbean but now live in England. In the first, the writer describes...

'Present from My Aunts in Pakistan'

Write three or four sentences about what the poet feels about her culture in this poem. Try to find at least one quotation as evidence.

'Hurricane Hits England'

Write three or four sentences about the culture the writer describes in this poem and her feelings about it. Try to find one quotation as evidence.

Structure

Write a sentence for each poem about how the poem is organised on the page and how this helps what the poets are saying.
For example, how each poem compares something in England with the same thing somewhere else.
Find one quotation as evidence.

Language

Write a sentence for each poem about the images used.
Find a quotation as evidence for each sentence.
Make sure you say how the image helps what the writer wants to say – does it suggest sadness, hope, memory?

Compare and contrast

Find at least one way in which the two poems are similar.
Find a quotation as evidence.
Write one way in which the two poems are different.
Find a quotation as evidence.

Conclusion

Finish with a paragraph summing up your main thoughts.
If possible, include something about your personal feelings about the poems, and how you relate to them.

2.17   A model response

Compare the importance of language to the poets in 'Search For My Tongue' and 'Unrelated Incidents'.

Look at the following. It provides a very broad basis for an essay on this subject. Read through the structure and then see how the paragraphs can be improved.

Introduction This contains one or two sentences that link the two poems together.	*The two poems 'Search For My tongue' and 'Unrelated Incidents' both explore how people relate to their mother tongue, and its power in enabling them to express themselves.*
First poem – 'Search For My Tongue' This paragraph needs to introduce the key 'story' of, or ideas behind 'Search For My Tongue'	*The poem 'Search For My Tongue' is about the two languages that Sujata Bhatt speaks. The poet's first language is Gujarati, her mother tongue. Her second language is English which she calls 'foreign'. She is proud of being able to use both languages, but finds there is a struggle between them.*
Second poem – 'Unrelated Incidents' This paragraph will move on to the second poem. It might refer to the first, but is likely to focus on the second.	*In Tom Leonard's poem, he seems to be saying that the television news needs to be read in more than one dialect or language. In fact, the poem is in the form of a broadcast. Usually the news is read using Standard English, but in the poem it is written using a Glasgow accent and dialect.*
Structure This paragraph needs to say something about the way the two poets have organised their ideas.	*'Search For My Tongue' is written in three stanzas to show the two different languages the poet speaks. It has one powerful image of a growing plant to show the importance of the poet's first language. 'Unrelated Incidents' is written as one stanza. There is also very little punctuation in the poem to make it sound like someone is speaking and to make a contrast with the formality of Standard English.*
Language This paragraph needs to say something about the way the two poets have used language to express their ideas.	*'Search For My Tongue' uses two languages to show how important they are to the poet, and develops the strong metaphor of the plant. 'Unrelated Incidents' uses the Glasgow dialect/accent and speaks directly, in plain language, to the reader – or listener. This shows how the news could be read in a different way.*
Compare and contrast This paragraph needs to give one or two similarities and one or two differences between the poems.	*The two poems are similar because they both use languages outside Standard English, but for different reasons. They both show that Standard English is not the only language, but one is concerned with the inner voice – your own tongue, and the other with the public voice and what should be heard. Tom Leonard uses a simple single stanza, whilst Sujata Bhatt employs three to show the different voices she uses.*
Conclusion Sum up by focusing on one or two key ideas, and perhaps expressing a personal opinion.	*Finally, I enjoyed reading both poems because they showed me how important the language I speak is to my identity. This is true both of the way we hear what we say in our heads, and how we are heard by others in public.*

2.18   There are no quotations in this first draft. Find one for each of the sections and decide how you could add it to the text.

Practice questions

Now you have worked through the selection of poems, here are four
possible questions you might face in the final exam.

If you are using these to help your revision, then follow this process:
- select the key words in the title
- reread the poems
- note down your first thoughts and impressions, including key words or lines
- write a brief plan (use the models on pages 89 and 102 if you wish)
- write your response.

**If you are using these as exam practice, remember that you will be choosing
one question, and will only have 45 minutes to finish your answer.
The exam will specify one poem you must refer to, and leave you to
choose the other (or others). Use the bullet points to guide you.**

1. Compare the presentation of different ways of life in 'What Were They Like?'
   and 'Two Scavengers in a Truck, Two Beautiful People in a Mercedes'.

Write about:
- the kinds of people described in each poem
- where they live
- the places and objects mentioned
- what these tell us about the people's lives.

2. Compare the use of contrasts to explain strong feelings in 'Nothing's Changed'
   and one other poem.

Write about:
- an explanation of the feelings expressed in each poem
- contrasts between the lives of black and white people in 'Nothing's Changed'
- contrasts used in the second poem you choose
- how these contrasts make you feel after reading both poems.

Practice questions cont.

---

3. Compare the way in which poets write about different languages or dialects in 'Search For My Tongue' and one other poem of your choice from the selection.

Write about:
*   the different people in the poems
*   the different languages used in the poems
*   what the poets feel about the languages being used
*   how the structure of each poem also shows what the poet feels about languages
*   your views on the poems.

4. Compare the ways in which poets from different cultures write about living in the United Kingdom in 'Hurricane Hits England' and one other poem of your choice from the selection.

Write about:
*   the different people in the poems and the cultures they belong to
*   the experiences these people have in the United Kingdom
*   how these experiences are similar or different to their experiences in another country
*   the way the poets use language to express their ideas
*   the way the poets have presented their poems
*   your views on the poems.

SUMMARY

*   Remember that the focus of the poems is on cultures and traditions – be clear what this means, and where they are described in the poems.

*   Prepare for the exam by making your own list of themes the examiner might want you to compare. Look for possible links between the poems.

*   Try to use a quotation (an actual word or phrase) from the poem for each point you make. Then write a sentence to explain how the quotation is linked to your point.

WRITING TO INFORM, EXPLAIN AND DESCRIBE

Introduction

The next three units will develop the writing skills required for one of the two writing sections of the exam. In the exam, you will have a choice of writing questions using these text types.

Where does this fit in the exam?

Paper 2 Section B

How long will I have?

You will have about 45 minutes to complete the work.

How will these units help?

Each unit deals with one of the text types in turn.

Read through this list of useful terms before you start this section.

abbreviated sentence	a short sentence or phrase in which the verb or other words are missing, for example 'easy to use' is short for 'it is easy to use'
first person	writing in which the narrator gives a personal view – he or she writes as 'I'
jargon	subject-specialised words or phrases that may be difficult for 'outsiders' to understand
opinion	a personal viewpoint or belief
technique	a skill needed for making your writing more effective
third person	writing when the writer uses the pronouns 'he', 'she', 'it', etc. This sometimes makes the text less personal (more impersonal)
topic sentence	key sentence (usually the first) in a paragraph

UNIT 1

WRITING TO INFORM

In this unit, you will:

- explore the skills you need to write in an informative way
- read a range of texts, all written to provide information
- complete tasks involving writing about computer viruses, tourist attractions, runaway children, product information, and much more.

You will learn how to:

- select the important facts and information needed in your writing
- provide explanations to support the facts
- present information in different ways and formats.

One key thing to remember:

- Writing to inform comes in many different forms, but it always provides facts in order to give the reader information.

Writing informative text

FACT

A **fact** is something that has actually occurred or can be proved to be true.

For example, it is a fact that you cannot take your driving test until you are 17.

.1

First, read this informative text.

> Cedar Point Amusement Park, Sandusky, Ohio, USA, which dates back to 1870, has 68 rides – more than any other single amusement or theme park. The park also has the most rollercoasters with 14 – two traditional wooden-track and 12 steel-track roller coasters featuring, among others, the 'Millennium Force', which opened in 2000 and is taller than the Statue of Liberty.
>
> *Guinness Book of Records 2002*

Make a list of all the facts in this entry. The first one is done for you.

● *Cedar Point Amusement Park has 68 rides*

● ....

● ....

.2

Now use the facts below to write a new entry for the *Guinness Book of Records.*

The title of the entry is: The Steepest Roller Coaster Ride

- The ride with the steepest drop is at Alton Towers theme park.
- The drop is 60 metres (197 ft long).
- The ride is called 'Oblivion'.
- The drop is 87.5 degrees.
- Passenger cars reach a speed of 70 mph.
- It is possible for 1,900 riders to ride every hour.

 Examiner's Tips

It is useful to start your entry with the most important fact. You can then use the other facts to give more information.

Here is another piece of informative writing.

> An estimated 100,000 under-16s go missing every year. One in three boys and one in five girls are under 11 when they first run away. Of this group 31 per cent have been excluded from school, 80 per cent are escaping from problems at home such as violence, abuse and conflict with parents, and 25 per cent end up sleeping rough. From the age of 14 upwards, girls are twice as likely to run away as boys, and 45 per cent of children in care run away compared with 9.5 per cent of those who live with their families. Abduction, while the most feared outcome for all people who go missing, is the least likely reason for absence.
>
> Schools could play a larger part in preventing children from running away. Children's problems often surface at school and that puts teachers on the front line. Given the right support and systems in schools, children at risk of running away can be identified before they feel the streets hold the only option for them.

There are **three** important things you need to notice about the way this piece is written.

1. It is **written in the third person** to make it less personal. It uses *'boys'*, *'girls'* and *'they'*.
2. It mainly **presents facts**.
3. It **makes a suggestion** that schools could do more to help children at risk of running away (so there is **advice** in the text, too).

1.3

Make a list of five facts that might persuade parents to attend a meeting about runaway children.

For example,

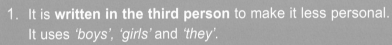

1. About 100,000 children under the age of 16 go missing each year.

Examiner's Tips

When writing to inform, it is your task to give the reader the information they need in order to make their own decision.

Using different forms of presentation

Now you are going to have a look at a completely different way of presenting information.

This information is:

- presented in the form of **a table**
- gives **facts** about a particular type of camera
- uses **headings** to make the information clear to the reader.

The information is presented in this way to help the reader decide whether a product suits their needs.

Price Band	Name/Price	Technical Data	Pros	Cons	Verdict/Score
Under £100	Coda 6X -5Y £79.99	35mm fully automatic lens-shutter. 70 mm lens. Electromagnetically driven shutter. Automatic film loading and winding. Frame counter.	Very clear picture in the viewfinder. Excellent manual controls. Good zoom quality. Easy to use. Good instructions.	Wide-angle lens aspect not very efficient. Quality of photographs variable even with recommended film.	Good for the price, but quality of photographs variable. 7/10

Look carefully at the language used in this table.

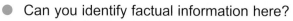

- Can you identify factual information here?
- Are there any special terms (jargon) in this text?
- Are there any examples of viewpoint or opinion? (Look for adjectives such as 'great' or 'bad'.)
- Are there any terms that could be both fact *and* opinion?

Now select a product from the list below. Complete a table like the one above for your product (choose at least one make or type):

- mobile phones
- televisions
- hair dryers
- skateboards
- roller blades

Examiner's Tips

When presenting information in a table, short, abbreviated sentences (such as 'good instructions' or '70mm lens') are quite acceptable.

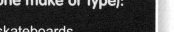

1.5

Read the following piece of text which informs you about some of the ways retailers encourage you to spend your money.

Note that this writing is arranged as a list of bullet points, each of which makes an individual point.

Ways to make you spend your money

- Supermarkets are the land that time forgot. The lack of clocks allows you to drift around, buying as much as possible.

- The smell of baking bread piped through a supermarket isn't your imagination – it's designed to whet your appetite for the food aisles.

- Children are a great weapon in the battle to keep you in the shop. One American supermarket uses a hopscotch game for kids on the floor of the cereal aisle so the parents browse there for longer.

- The bright lights in the supermarket health and beauty aisle are designed to remind you of the chemist and a clinical atmosphere.

- The food court in shopping malls is always at the top of the building so you pass as many shops as possible on the way there. There are escalators to take you up, but rarely back down again.

- Traditionally, men stop women spending money. So comfortable chairs, like the sofas in the Bluewater shopping centre, are designed so that men can wait until the shopping trip is over.

- As you pause to admire yourself in a strategically placed mirror of a department store, you are actually being offered a chance to see more products on which to spend cash.

- It seems that the product you want is always in easy reach of your right hand, but the right-hand side of the shelf is where shops deliberately put the products they're really trying to sell.

.6

Here are four pieces of advice based on the information.
Find the relevant bullet point for each.

The first example has been done for you.

Advice	Information
• Always take a watch when you go shopping. Supermarkets don't have clocks and you don't want to waste time.	• Supermarkets are the land that time forgot. The lack of clocks allows you to drift around, buying as much as possible.
• Ignore delicious smells!	•
• Don't get too comfortable in any easy chairs – you'll stay longer.	•
• Keep away from mirrors. They just show you more products!	•

Answering the questions, 'What?' and 'How?'

.7

You are now going to read two texts that give information about
infections and how we can prevent them.

The first informs people about immunisation, which protects people from
illness and disease. **The second** tells us about viruses in computers and
how we can prevent them.

Notice the way the texts answer the questions, 'What?' and 'How?'.

 Examiner's Tips

Sub-headings and punctuation marks are often used to
organise and structure a piece of writing.

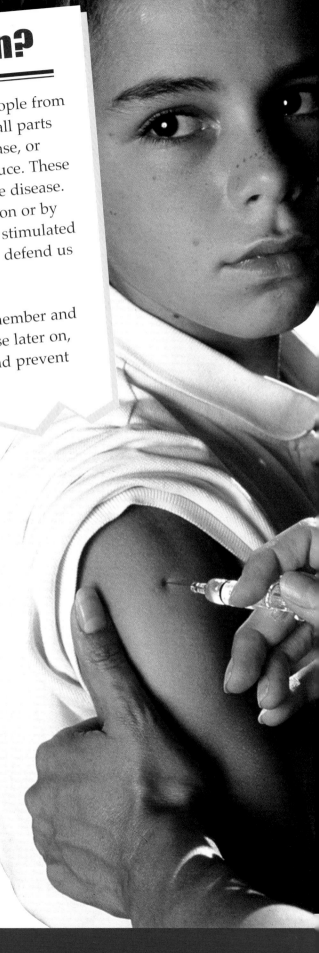

What is **Immunisation?**

Immunisation is using a vaccine to protect people from getting a disease. Vaccines contain either small parts of the viruses or bacteria which cause the disease, or very small amounts of the chemical they produce. These have been treated so that they do not cause the disease. When we are given a vaccine, either by injection or by mouth (as with polio vaccine), our bodies are stimulated to make substances called antibodies – which defend us against future infections.

Our bodies make special cells which can remember and recognise infections, so if we meet the disease later on, the body's defences (the antibodies) fight and prevent the infection from getting a hold.

1.8

Now you have read the information about immunisation, answer the questions below in your words:

- What is immunisation?
- What is a vaccine?
- How do vaccines work, at first?
- How do vaccines work, later on?

Notice that the passage is written in the **first person**, using 'we' and 'our'.

The piece you are about to read on computer viruses uses both the **third person**, using 'they' and the **second person**, using 'you'.

You will have to decide which is the most appropriate when you do your own informative writing.

Now read this text about computer viruses and what we can do to prevent them.

What are Computer Viruses?

Introduction

It seems that all through the year people are concerned with infections and viruses. Immunisations are given to babies and young children, injections are given to people travelling abroad and the simple flu jab to adults as winter approaches. These are all measures taken to stop people getting ill. However, it is not just people who suffer from nasty bugs, the virtual world also has its own infections. Computer viruses are everywhere. So what is a computer virus?

What is a computer virus?

Like infections in people, computer infections or viruses take a variety of forms. Some viruses 'piggyback' on program files, infecting everything in sight when the program software is started up. Other viruses hide away in the computer's start up data and memory waiting for a specific day, date or time to do their dirty work. Another type of virus is called a 'Trojan'. This type of virus disguises itself as something else, maybe a computer game and then once loaded it interferes with the computer's workings, erasing the hard disk, for example, or sending silly messages. There are many types of virus but they all share the common trait of being able to reproduce themselves and spread.

What is the most common form of computer virus today?

This is through email or through email attachments. Open the email attachment and you have infected your computer. Often these viruses are designed to take all the email addresses from your computer and forward themselves to all your friends and colleagues. The virus pretends to be a message from yourself. Sometimes a hoax virus is sent. This is usually sent as an email warning of a virus which is going around. It advises that the warning is passed on. Thus the hoax virus is propagated or spread.

Who creates a computer virus?

Virus writers are responsible for creating computer viruses. Increasingly they are setting out to cause serious damage. They want to destroy valuable data and to spread a virus from computer to computer as quickly and efficiently as possible.

How can computer viruses be stopped?

It is important that a computer is loaded with an anti-virus software application in order to fight off any electronic viruses which might come their way. It is also important to be aware that floppy disks carry a risk of infection.

1.9   You are now going to write an informative email that answers the questions 'what' and 'how'.

An adult in your family has bought a second-hand computer, but doesn't know much about computers and how to use them. You have realised the computer needs to be loaded with anti-virus software. Write an email welcoming your relative to the world of computers.

In it you will tell them about anti-virus software and why they need to invest in it.

Try to compare the treatment of human viruses with computer viruses to help the adult understand what a computer virus is.

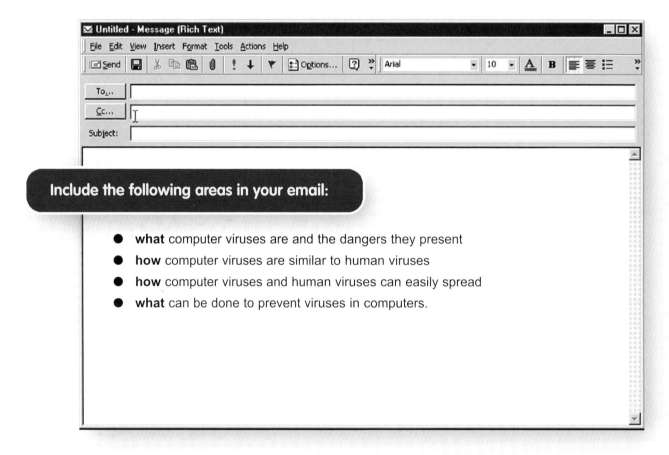

Include the following areas in your email:

- **what** computer viruses are and the dangers they present
- **how** computer viruses are similar to human viruses
- **how** computer viruses and human viruses can easily spread
- **what** can be done to prevent viruses in computers.

 Examiner's Tips

In this piece of writing you need to give the facts and then explain these facts in order to inform your relative.

Again, this is similar to writing to advise, but the key is to give them the information they need to make their own decision.

1.10 Use the skills developed in this unit to answer this practice question.

Your school is involved in an exchange with pupils from another country.
Your teacher has asked you to contribute to a booklet which will inform the visitors about how they might enjoy themselves in the United Kingdom.

The booklet will contain sections on:

- good television programmes to watch
- good films around at the moment
- good places to visit in the local area
- what they need to know about getting around
- signs, signals and useful phrases.

Choose **one or more** of the sections above and write your contribution to the booklet.

SUMMARY

- Informative writing lets the reader make decisions.
- It can be presented in many different ways.
- You should be clear about what is fact and what is opinion.
- Your goal is to increase a reader's knowledge – so explain your information.
- Most informative writing answers the questions 'What?' and 'How?'.

UNIT 2

WRITING TO EXPLAIN

In this unit, you will:

- explore skills needed when you write explanations
- read and study an article about Garage music, and user notes for a new computer game
- read and write about personal beliefs.

You will learn how to:

- write in appropriate detail
- make your ideas crystal clear.

One key thing to remember:

- writing to explain means explaining something known to you, but not to others, which may be complicated or difficult to understand.

An explanation could be:

- a **process** – how I became President of the USA
- an **emotion** – how I felt when I accepted my Oscar
- a **belief** – why I am a vegetarian
- a **person** – who is the mysterious neighbour in our road
- an **event** – what happened the day we moved house.

Identifying explanations

.1

Read through the explanations below.

> When my son was born I felt so excited I thought I was going to burst with happiness. How can you explain happiness? I guess it's a light-headed feeling, as if you are dancing on air.

> Getting five stars in the FA soccer skills programme was not easy. It began with hours of practice: dribbling through the cones, shuttle runs, having to hit the target with my left and right feet, and lots more. Then there were the Saturday mornings standing in the rain waiting my turn, and then, finally, the announcement I had been waiting for.

> My best friend in Southampton likes exactly the same things as me. She's into R'n'B and likes going off all day long on her bike. When we get together we just disappear off on our own and talk about everything under the sun. I expect you have friends just like this. If you do, you're lucky.

> We lock far too many people up. I have always believed this, and I still do now. Throughout the world I have protested against heavy sentences, especially for young people. I suppose it all started when my own brother was sent to a Young Offender's Institution.

> My 16th birthday was a great occasion. We hired a big hall, and all my friends came. Mum ordered pizzas, and we chose the music.

Identify which of the explanations has most to do with:

- a process
- an emotion
- a belief
- a person
- an event.

 Which of them have a mixture of these things?

Read the extract below. It was written in the late 1990s. Kate Lloyd, a teenage writer from Hackney, East London, explains some of the features of her favourite style of music, 'Garage'.

It's a Garage T'ing

At the moment I'm really into Garage music. I can't describe the feeling I get when a wicked tune comes on. I get shivers down my spine... You don't have to know who the MC is, you just need to enjoy yourself. It's jump up! You *have* to dance to it, even if your only dance floor is your bedroom. After all, what else is a girl who listens to Garage supposed to do?

Garage has taken over the London dance scene. It is characterised by rhythmic basslines, catchy melodies and soulful singing. It has actually been around for years, with its roots in an American club called 'The Garage'. Technically it is 'house with soul' and even though British clubbers were already listening to it by the early nineties, the scene did not really kick off until the rise of 'UK Garage' a few years ago.

Sadly Girl Power hasn't really hit Garage yet. This is made perfectly clear by the professionally printed fliers with half-naked women adorning them. Women – or should I say 'Laydeeez' – are still expected to dress up to the nines in high heels and short skirts and to dance for men. It's not all bad though. You get into clubs cheaper and usually there's someone desperate to buy you a drink. We're not stupid; we just take advantage of the blatant sexism – now there's girl power for you!

British Garage has been getting better and better in recent years but it's also becoming more commercial. The media quickly pick up on what's happening underground and know exactly how to make money out of it, putting out shows and advertising raves on Teletext. Certain raves and club nights are hyped, with guest DJs and promoters using the media to advertise themselves. What a change from the time when the only way to find out which DJs would be there was by listening to pirate stations – that was a lot more exciting!

Ordering information

2

Read through the following list of points and try to put them into the order that Kate has used.

- Girl fans of Garage music are expected to dress up to please men.
- The success of Garage has meant that it has become more commercial.
- Garage music is special because it makes you want to get up and dance.
- Women fans do get some advantages from the sexism which is part of the club scene. For instance, they get cheaper entry into clubs.
- Nowadays, the music is hyped by the mainstream media.
- It all started in an American club called 'The Garage'.
- The music has been known in Britain since the early nineties.
- Technically it is 'house with soul'.

 Is the information well organised?

Using paragraphs

Kate has also used **paragraphs** to group her ideas even more clearly.

3

Make up a title for each of the four paragraphs in the extract.

For example, you could call the first paragraph

'What's So Good About Garage Music?'.

Using informal language

2.4

In some parts of her explanation, Kate has used informal language, and language specific to 'Garage' music. This shows that she knows about Garage music, and is on the same level as her readers.

- Find and write down **five** examples of this, and explain what each means.

Copy and complete this table:

Informal language	Meaning
I'm really into	I very much enjoy
wicked bass-lines	

Organising an explanation

2.5

Think carefully about your own favourite type of music.

It could be anything, for example:
- military brass band marches
- traditional music of a country you know and love
- the very latest pop music
- electronic inventions
- something so new that hardly anyone has heard of it yet.

Write a short explanation like Kate's. First, think up a good title that tells your readers the name of the musical style you're writing about.

- In the first paragraph, explain why this music is special to you.
- In the second paragraph, explain what it is like and how it is different from other types.
- In the third paragraph, explain how it has developed.

Write about half a page.
You may like to use the writing frame on the opposite page.

The music I'm really into is...

It is special to me because...

The music is characterised by...

It has been around for...

Fans are expected to wear...

It has its roots in...

Nowadays...

If you have trouble describing your favourite style of music and its background in this sort of detail, write about a favourite sport – or one you know well. You could include the same information:

- what the sport is
- why you like it
- what its special features (characteristics) are
- its history (if you know it)
- its importance today.

 Examiner's Tips

Use **different** paragraphs for **different** purposes: to define the thing you are describing, to give examples and so on.

2.6

Below, you will find CD notes for a new computer game called 'Oceanplanet'.

Before you start reading, make a list of questions you would ask to find out about a new computer game, for example, 'Where does it take place?' (its territory).

Playing 'Oceanplanet'

Oceanplanet is a blue, underwater world. To explore it, you won't need wheels, an engine or an airline ticket – just your computer mouse and a powerful imagination.

Part of the fun of this game lies in discovering the many secrets of the planet itself. There's a lot to find out and the convincing graphics are full of surprises. Moving around is simple. The mouse pointer becomes a small pilot fish, which you simply position where you want to go, and click. So wherever you find yourself, you have the ability to navigate out of trouble.

So what is the point of Oceanplanet? As in most fantasy games, the player quickly becomes involved in a battle of Good against Evil. You are Bluefin, a member of a highly intelligent troupe of dolphinoids. Your task is to confront the powerful forces which seek to destroy Oceanplanet.

In this game, enemies come thick and fast and it is important to learn their names and powers as quickly as possible. Stink–worms or Fire–squids can attack at any time! A quick click will open one of the clamshells clustered on the rocks at the bottom of the screen. They are there to guide you, and are packed with vital information about the powers and weaknesses of the Evil Ones.

As the game progresses, players' missions and roles change. Each task can be carried out in different ways. Problem solving can earn you an undersea shuttle–ride, or you might find yourself leading an attack on the Fire–squids in their undersea volcanic caves.The action can get pretty fast, and very destructive.

At the end of a game, successful players have the chance to free Oceanplanet from the Evil Ones. New areas of the planet are revealed, with some brilliant, white–knuckle special effects. You're probably wondering what these are – but that would be telling! Oceanplanet's secrets are there to be discovered – but only by the most adventurous players.

How many of your questions were answered?
Tick them.

 Is it a good explanation or are there some gaps?

.7 How has the writer organised his explanation
and made it clear and easy to understand?

> **Number each paragraph and then choose a
> name for each one from this list:**
>
> - The Point of the Game
> - The End of the Game
> - What is Oceanplanet?
> - Enemies and Helpers
> - Travelling Around the Planet
> - Roles and Structure.

.8 Look at the techniques listed in the table below.
These all help to improve the explanation.

Find three examples from the text for each technique.
Some have already been done for you

Techniques used	Examples from the text	How does this improve the explanation?
The second person	• **You** won't need wheels, an engine or an airline ticket • •	It makes the readers feel more involved because the writer is talking directly to them.
The present tense	• • •	This tells us that we are reading an explanation, not a story or a piece of history. It makes it clear that the game exists now.
Connectives	• … a world of beauty **but also** of secrets… • **As** the game progresses •	These link ideas in various ways, indicating the sequence of events, a contrast or an addition.
Topic sentences	• • •	These sentences (the first of each paragraph) introduce the topic of the paragraph.
The writer goes into detail by answering questions like **When?** **Where?** **How?**	• At the end of a game… • … clustered on the rocks •	These answer the questions that players might want to ask.

Now look at this advert from a local paper.

Are You Still At School Or College?
Do You Believe In God?

University researcher seeks young people prepared to talk in detail about their religious beliefs. Believers and non-believers are equally welcome.

Financial reward available!

Please send in a short account (200–300 words) explaining your beliefs.

I am interested in:

- your own religious beliefs (explain these in detail)
- the influence of your family, friends or school
- what you think have been the strongest influences on your religious beliefs.

You decide to answer the advert. The financial reward sounds tempting!

Writing a formal explanation

.9

For this task, you are telling a stranger about your views.
Start with the first bullet point in the advert.

In a pair or small group, practise explaining your own views to some of your friends.
If you like, use one of the following starters:

- I've always believed in God. It's very important to me because...

- My religion is... It means that I believe in...

- I've never really believed in God, but I do believe in...

Listen to what your friends have to say, and help them to say
more by asking questions.

Here's one example, written by a pupil who isn't sure about her beliefs.
See how many of the techniques from the table on page 123 she has used.

I can't really describe my religious beliefs. I do want to believe that there is more to life than just what you can see in front of your eyes or on the news. Also, I strongly believe in right and wrong. For instance, I can't stand it when people are cruel to animals, especially dogs. However, no one I know has a religion or goes to church, except my grandad. I was once told that the word for someone who isn't sure about their religion is an agnostic. So I suppose I am an agnostic.

> Next, write one paragraph on 'My Beliefs'. Use:
>
> - a **topic sentence**
> - the **present tense**
> - some **connectives** (so, because, however etc.).

Unpacking your ideas

Think of an idea as being like a suitcase. When it is closed, it looks like just one thing. But when you open it up, you might find all kinds of things inside.

Here's what one pupil wrote for the second bullet point in the advert (its influence):

> It's hard for me because my family is very religious but none of my friends are. I don't know if either of them have influenced me.

2.10

Try these three ways to help him to 'unpack' his statement. Copy out his words and then write more.

1. Give an example. Start a new sentence with 'For example...'
   Imagine and then describe a very religious member of his family.

2. Give a contrasting example. Start another sentence with 'On the other hand...'
   Imagine and describe a friend who thinks that religion is boring and pointless.

3. Explain how this has affected him. Start a third sentence with 'The result of this is...'

Here is another example of a paragraph about the possible influence of family. For Tahira's father, religion meant something rather different!

> Both my parents are Muslims, but sometimes my father talks about religion in a different way. He talks as if football were a religion! He claims that football can break down barriers and unite complete strangers. I must admit that this has had an influence on me. I've always been a Sheffield Wednesday fan. I wouldn't describe any footballer as God, but I do think that the spiritual alignment you see when the team is winning has to be a gift from God.

.11

Now write your own response.

> ### Write the 200–300 word account asked for in the advert.
>
> ● Write one paragraph for each bullet point.
> ● You can make it informative, thoughtful, or even funny.
> ● Unpack each of your ideas so that the researcher can understand **exactly** what's inside each one.
> ● Use connectives to make links between one idea and the next.

.12

Use the skills developed in this unit to answer this practice question.

You have been asked to help create the exhibits for a Museum of the Twenty-First Century. The idea is that people in the future will be able to come along and see what life was like in your times.

Your task is to:
● pick one machine which you think is a good example of the best aspects of the technologies we have available in our society
● write a detailed explanation (about 250 words) to go next to your exhibit.

Explain:
● what it is
● what it can do/how it is used/what kinds of people use it
● when and how it was first made (if you know)
● why it is so excellent.

SUMMARY

● 'Unpack your ideas' with examples to make your explanation clear.
● Focus on paragraphs for individual points.
● Show connections, causes and effects through link words.

UNIT 3 — WRITING TO DESCRIBE

In this unit, you will:

- explore how writers use a variety of ways to describe people, places or experiences
- read a number of pieces of descriptive writing
- complete tasks that will help you to write in a more interesting way.

You will learn how to:

- vary the length and type of sentences
- use paragraphs to organise and clarify
- compare experiences to make your writing more powerful
- use dialogue and metaphor to make your writing interesting
- focus on powerful verbs.

One key thing to remember:

- writing to describe will *show rather than tell* your reader if you use powerful, strong words.

Read this descriptive piece by former footballer Gary Mabbutt. Here, he describes his experience of becoming a father for the first time.

I am always being asked what was the best day of my life. Winning the Uefa cup? Playing for England? Captaining Tottenham for 11 years or winning the FA cup? In my professional career, I was very fortunate to realise a lot of my ambitions. Lifting the FA cup at Wembley in 1991 as the victorious captain was definitely a very emotional moment. But nothing compared to the emotions I felt when I saw my daughter for the first time.

Overnight, my attitude to the most important things in my life, and all my priorities have changed. Having played most of my career as a defender, I thought that I was more than capable of dealing with players dribbling, being thrown a dummy and being forced to clean up at the back by my opponents, but all these incidents suddenly took on a new significance.

During my career, I prided myself on my positional sense and my ability to keep my opponents under close surveillance. Marking players such as Gary Lineker, Michael Owen and Alan Shearer meant you had to concentrate for every second of the game. In a shopping situation, Stephanie (my daughter) is in the same league as my old adversaries: she will drift on to my blind side and, if I have a moment of hesitation, she is gone, goodness knows where. Dad's complete panic is relieved only when she jumps out from under the stack of cornflakes with a "peek-a-boo".

Gary was known as a brave player.
Here, he wears a face mask to protect a serious injury.

Using comparisons

3.1   Gary Mabbutt compares his experience as a professional footballer with that of being a father.

What experiences as a footballer does he refer to?

Read the second paragraph and find two or three expressions or words which are used in football and could also refer to looking after a young child.

Look at how he *shows* his daughter's behaviour as well as telling us what it is like being a father.

3.2   Think of an experience that you have had which is – or was – very important to you. Then, think of another experience of lesser importance.

For example, you could compare your first day at secondary school with your first day on work experience.

Write **one** or **two** paragraphs in which you describe the experience you had, give a detail from the experience, and show why it is – or was – so important.

Examiner's Tips

Comparing experiences is a good way to give an interesting structure to your writing.

Now read this piece by World War One veteran Harry Patch.
He is describing an experience that happened more than 80 years ago.

We were part of the battalion, but at the same time we were a little crowd on our own. We lived hour to hour, and everything we had was shared. My mother used to send me a parcel once a fortnight. In that parcel was an ounce of tobacco, two packets of cigarettes, a few sweets and cakes, a couple of socks. That ounce of tobacco was cut in half – number three had half, I had half. The cigarettes were divided among the other three, 13 each. They used to take it in turns who would get the odd one. Everything was shared. They died on September 22 and for me that is remembrance day.

Harry Patch uses a small example (the shared cigarettes and tobacco) to show a bigger idea (how much he valued his friends during this time).

Here is another example of this. In it a 15-year-old pupil describes the importance of friendship to her. Can you spot the 'small example' here?

We were on our way back from Alton Towers and I only had a bag of crisps left but some of my friends had other things, like chocolate, Skittles, an orange and more crisps. We sat at the back of the coach and got out all our stuff, we said that we might as well share it otherwise it was going to be a boring journey back, and so we did. It was much more fun than just sitting and eating the same old bag of boring crisps. Even one or two boys who never normally speak to us came and joined in!

3.3

Think of a time when a small event, or moment, showed the importance of friendship to you.

Write a paragraph describing the incident in a similar way to Harry Patch and the school pupil. Remember to include at least one detail.

Examiner's Tips

Both Harry Patch and the girl use **lists of nouns** in their writing. Using lists of nouns can emphasise a point. It can also give you a different type of sentence.

This next example of descriptive writing is about **a person, a place** and **an experience**.

The extract gives an account of the writer's first visit to the UK from America. He is sleeping rough on a bench. This is the first of two extracts from the same book.

Extract 1

Further along Marine Parade stood a shelter, open to the elements but roofed, and I decided that this was as good as I was going to get. With my backpack for a pillow, I lay down and drew my jacket tight around me. The bench was slatted and hard and studded with big roundheaded bolts that made reclining in comfort an impossibility – doubtless their intention. I lay for a long time listening to the sea washing over the shingle below, and eventually dropped off to a long, cold night of mumbled dreams…

I awoke with a gasp about three, stiff all over and quivering from cold. The fog had gone. The air was now still and clear, and the sky was bright with stars. A beacon from the lighthouse at the far end of the backwater swept endlessly over the sea. It was all most fetching, but I was far too cold to appreciate it. I dug shiveringly through my backpack and extracted every potentially warming item I could find – a flannel shirt, two sweaters, an extra pair of jeans. I used some woollen socks as mittens and put a pair of flannel boxer shorts on my head as a kind of desperate headwarmer, then sank heavily back onto the bench and waited patiently for death's sweet kiss. Instead, I fell asleep.

Bill Bryson

Using different types of sentence

.4

Write down the two shortest sentences Bill Bryson uses. Notice how these draw attention to the subject of the sentence because they are short.

For example   *'The fog had gone.'*

This type of sentence is called a **simple sentence**, and makes sense on its own. It consists of a **noun** (the subject – fog), and a **verb** (had gone).

Another type of sentence is a **compound sentence**. This contains two or more simple sentences joined together.

For example   *'The air was still and the sky was bright.'*

In this example, **and** joins the two simple sentences together.

A **complex sentence** is one that contains a **main clause** and a **subordinate clause**.

main clause		subordinate clause

For example   ***'Further along Marine Parade stood a shelter, open to the elements but roofed,** and I decided that this was as good as I was going to get.'*

In this sentence, the extra information about the shelter is separated by the use of commas.

Bill Bryson could have used 'which' or 'that'.

For example 'Further along Marine Parade stood a shelter, **which** was leaking badly.'

This works for descriptions of people, too.

.5

Can you identify the simple and complex sentences in these lines?

He stands, waiting, by the window. A smell of dust lingers in the room. The moon, bright on the horizon but distant, hangs like a ring of ice. He waits for Death, which will bring him Life.

 Examiner's Tips

Appealing to the readers' senses can also help your descriptive writing. What two senses are used in the lines above?

Now read a second extract from Bill Bryson's account.

Extract 2

I was awakened again by an abrupt bellow of foghorn, which nearly knocked me from my narrow perch, and sat up feeling wretched but fractionally less cold. The world was bathed in that milky pre-dawn light that seems to come from nowhere. Gulls wheeled and cried over the water. Beyond them, past the stone breakwater, a ferry, vast and well lit, slid regally out to sea. I sat there for some time, a young man with more on his mind than in it. Another booming moan from the ship's foghorn passed over the water, re-exciting the irksome gulls. I took off my sock mittens and looked at my watch. It was 5.55 a.m. I looked at the receding ferry and wondered where anybody would be going at that hour. Where would *I* go at that hour? I picked up my backpack and shuffled off down the prom, to get some circulation going.

Near the Churchill [a hotel], now itself peacefully sleeping, I came across an old guy walking a little dog. The dog was frantically trying to pee on every vertical surface and in consequence wasn't so much walking as being dragged along on three legs.

The man nodded a good-morning as I drew level. 'Might turn out nice,' he announced, gazing hopefully at a sky that looked like a pile of wet towels. I asked him if there was a restaurant anywhere that might be open. He knew of a place not far away and directed me to it. 'Best transport caff in Kent,' he said.

'Transport calf?,' I repeated uncertainly, and retreated a couple of paces as I'd noticed his dog was straining desperately to moisten my leg.

'Very popular with the lorry drivers. They always know the best places, don't they?' He smiled amiably, then lowered his voice a fraction and leaned towards me as if about to share a confidence. 'You might want to take them pants off your head before you go in.'

I clutched my head – 'Oh!' – and removed the forgotten boxer shorts with a blush. I tried to think of a succinct explanation, but the man was scanning the sky again.

'Definitely brightening up,' he decided, and dragged his dog off in search of new uprights. I watched them go, then turned and walked off down the promenade as it began to spit with rain.

Using dialogue and humour

The writer uses dialogue in this piece to introduce a character whom he meets when he wakes up.

He is also able to make the meeting funny because of the behaviour of the dog and the incident with his boxer shorts. Again, detail is used to make the piece come to life.

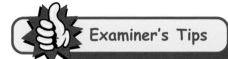

Examiner's Tips

Keep your reader interested in your writing.
Adding dialogue can make it more interesting – and funny,
as can small details of behaviour.

3.6 **Imagine the old man continues on his way, walking his dog.
He meets a friend and describes for him the encounter he has just had.**

Write the conversation the two men might have. Try to include further description between the speech. You might begin like this…

'Morning Joe, I've just met the strangest man back there.'
The man with the dog halted once again, by a road-sign.
'Oh, morning, Will. What do you mean, strange?'

Using metaphor

A **metaphor** is a word or phrase used to describe something as if it were something else. This can emphasise a particular characteristic.

For example 'Gulls wheeled'

Gulls are birds and do not have 'wheels'. They have wings. But the writer uses the word 'wheeled' to *emphasise* the circular motion the gulls are making in the sky, like wheels.

3.7 **Copy and complete the following table. It gives examples of the way the writer has used metaphor in both extracts.**

Object being described	Metaphorical word or phrase
ship's foghorn	moan
rain	
	bathed
	sweet kiss

Using powerful verbs

It is important to make your verbs (words of action or being) as strong as possible. Some of these have already come up as part of the work on metaphor.

The vast army **swarmed** over the rocks, **beetling** up the rocky crags. Their enemies **slunk** back into their caves, or when caught **pleaded** for mercy. None was given.

 Look back at Bill Bryson's writing. Are there any strong verbs in the first extract?

3.8 Write a 100-word description of someone who is to be found in an unusual place. For example, a great grandfather at a night-club, or a small child in a forest. Use powerful verbs to describe the place – and person.

3.9 Use the skills developed in this unit to answers this practice question.

Describe a day out that you have enjoyed. You will need to show exactly what it was that made this particular day so enjoyable.

You should aim to include a description of the following:

- the journey
- the place
- the person or people you went with
- what you did
- why it was so special.

SUMMARY

- A variety of sentences, simple and complex, can improve description.
- Effective paragraphs make effective description.
- Strong verbs, and lists of nouns, can make writing vivid.
- Use of dialogue, and humour, can give variety and interest.
- You can write about people, places, processes, events or emotions when describing.

PRACTICE PAPER

In this final section of the book, you will have a chance to work through a full practice paper based on the exam you will take.

For the reading section:

- establish audience and purpose
- focus on fact and opinion
- consider similarities and differences
- consider layout and presentation
- back up your ideas with quotations and examples.

For the writing sections use the writing process:

- generate/list ideas
- sort your ideas into order
- jot down key phrases, or sentences you want to use
- write your draft
- check your writing.

For the poetry section:

- look for links between poems
- consider differences and similarities
- look for powerful images and lines
- back up your ideas with quotations or examples
- use poetic terms, and explain their effect.

General advice:

- read all questions carefully
- identify the key words in the title
- stick to what you should be writing about
- use organisational words ('however', 'as a result' etc)
- where appropriate, give your personal views
- use a plan and stick to it.

ENGLISH A
Paper 1

Time allowed: 1 hour 45 minutes

SECTION A: READING

Answer **all** the questions in this Section.
Spend about **60 minutes** on this Section.

**Read the article 'Fit to drop' by Chris Harris.
It is about the problems with exercise.**

You are being asked to follow an argument and tell fact from opinion.

1(a) Write down **two** facts about swimming mentioned in the article.   (2 marks)

1(b) Explain in your own words why Chris Harris is against exercise.   (4 marks)

For this question, you are asked to compare the newspaper article and the magazine front cover.

1(c) Compare the ideas about the value of sport and fitness presented in the newspaper article and the magazine cover.
Write about:
- the language used in each text
- what each text says you can gain from knowing more about sport and fitness.   (7 marks)

Now read the magazine cover as a media text.

2(a) How do the visual images and layout help:
- to make the magazine look exciting
- to attract readers?   (7 marks)

2(b) Choose and write down **three** examples of language used on the magazine cover and for each one explain how it helps to attract the target audience (male readers who would like to get fit).   (7 marks)

Total: 27 marks

SECTION B: WRITING TO ARGUE, PERSUADE OR ADVISE

Answer **one** question in this Section.
Spend about **45 minutes** on this Section.
You may use some of the information from Section A if you want to,
but you do not have to do so.
If you use any of the information do not simply copy it.

> **Remember:**
> - spend 5 minutes planning and sequencing your material
> - try to write at least two sides
> - spend 5 minutes checking your:
>   - paragraphing
>   - punctuation
>   - spelling.

Either

3. Imagine you are the parent of a secondary school pupil. Write a letter to your son or daughter's headteacher in which you:

    (a) **argue** that body-building should be included as one of the sports taught at the school

    (b) **persuade** the head to appoint a new teacher to set up an after-school body-building club.

    (27 marks)

    Remember to:
    - set your writing out as a letter
    - write as if you were a parent writing to the headteacher
    - give several points to back up your argument and to persuade the headteacher.

(see Questions 4 and 5 overleaf)

Or

4. Write the text for a speech in which you **argue** that there is a lot more to life than building up your muscles. (27 marks)

   Remember to:
   ● aim your speech at a specific audience
   ● include more than one argument.

Or

5. Write an article for a school magazine, giving year 7 pupils **advice** on staying safe on the streets of your town or local area. (27 marks)

   Remember to:
   ● set your writing out as an article
   ● write for year 7 pupils
   ● concentrate on what they need to know to stay safe.

ENGLISH A
Paper 2

Time allowed: 1 hour 30 minutes

SECTION A: READING

This section relates to Section 1 of the 2004 AQA Anthology
that you have used during the course.
Answer **one** question from this Section on the poems you have studied.
Spend about **45 minutes** on this section.

Either

1. Compare 'Two Scavengers in a Truck' with **one** other poem of your choice from this selection. Show how the poets present their ideas and feelings about life in a big city.

    Write about:
    ● what each city is like
    ● what the poets think and feel about each city
    ● how the language and presentation of each poem makes these ideas
       and feelings clear.   (27 marks)

Or

2. Compare the ways in which the poets explore the experience of prejudice in 'Unrelated Incidents' and **one** other poem.

    Write about:
    ● the kind of prejudice described in each poem
    ● each poet's use of personal examples to show the effects of prejudice
    ● how the poets use language and layout to present their views in a powerful way.
                                                                        (27 marks)

FIT TO DROP

People who exercise are always ill, says Chris Harris

I went to a meal at a friend's house the other day and was surprised to find I was the only guest there. When I questioned my host he told me that Isobel had strained her neck doing weight-training at the gym, Phil had caught flu while doing a half-marathon in driving rain, and Sam was doubtful as a result of the black eye someone had given him in a football match. When I pointed out that this surely didn't prevent him coming for dinner, my friend said that Sam was too embarrassed to be seen with it, in case anyone thought his girlfriend had done it!

All this proves what I have known for a long time: exercise makes you ill. Provided you don't eat takeaways every night and make sure you go for the occasional stroll to the shops rather than hop in the car, then you will live a long and injury-free existence. Even a seemingly innocuous activity such as swimming can be dangerous. Just think – the average adult human head weighs about 10lb, so holding it above the water puts a fantastic load on the shoulders. Ah, I hear you say, but good swimmers put their heads in the water. Yes, I answer, but water contains chlorine, and just think of all that chlorine in your hair and eyes – not to mention what other swimmers may have done… if you get my meaning. If God had wanted us to be fish, he would have given us fins, scales, and tails that could wiggle from side to side.

When I was young, of course, I didn't know any better, and at first, I took part in all sorts of sporting activities: football, basketball, cricket, rugby… you name it, I did it. The problem was that although I did all these sports, I was still tall, pale and skinny. It might have been OK if I'd been a brilliant guitar player, or a moody lead singer, or even a passionate animal rights activist. But I wasn't. I was just an ordinary teenager who wanted girls to fancy him.

So, I joined the school body-building club, which was full of tall, pale and skinny boys just like me. For six months, I turned up hoping I would be transformed into Mr Universe, or Russell Crowe at least, but all I got were sore arms, an aching back, and the leftovers from dinner (we were always last into the dinner queue). Even if I had developed bulging biceps, no one would have noticed; it was so cold in our school even the radiators had frost on them, and no one in his right mind took his jumper off.

It wasn't until I was much older that I realised that many body-builders took food supplements, steroids and other additives to boost their pecs. I also read an article about the same time describing body-builders who had become ill and had heart problems because of these supplements, or so the article claimed.

Today, I don't have to worry about being skinny – I have the perfect appearance for a man of my age (a slightly plump stomach, and a balding head), and I am rarely ill. I avoid swimming pools, fitness clubs, tennis courts, public parks and fun-runs. I tried cycling once, and the exercise was quite pleasant. However, the fact that enormous lorries seemed to enjoy forcing me off my bike into people's front gardens rather put me off. Nowadays, my main exercise is a wander round the garden to snip a few roses, and the odd bit of typing on my computer. Come to think of it, my wrist is hurting. Perhaps I have got repetitive strain injury. Who knows? It's a dangerous world we live in.

FREE £5 VOUCHER FOR EVERY READER p.63

Joe Weider's

FLEX ®

GET HUGE!

MR. OLYMPIA'S PROGRAMME FOR SIZE & POWER
How It Can Work For *YOU!*
page 16

GIANT TRAPS
How To Build 'Em
page 68

CUTTING EDGES
9 Surprising Fat-Burning Supplements! page 96

BIG BICEPS!
The 5 Exercises You Need! page 50

www.flexonline.com

February 2002 £3.25

02

9 770955 121068

Breaking Research

THE BEST PROTEIN SOURCE!
page 60

143

SECTION B: WRITING TO INFORM, EXPLAIN OR DESCRIBE

Answer **one** question in this Section.
Spend about **45 minutes** on this Section.

> **Remember:**
>
> - Spend 5 minutes planning and sequencing your material
> - Try to write at least two sides
> - Spend 5 minutes checking your:
>   - paragraphing
>   - punctuation
>   - spelling.

Either

3. Choose a book or a TV series you know well.
    Write an **informative** article about it for a teenage magazine.
    Include information about:
    - the content
    - the place or places in which it is set
    - the characters or people involved
    - an example of a typical event or incident
    - why teenagers might enjoy it.   (27 marks)

Or

4. Sometimes, the support of a friend or family member can be very helpful.
    Think of a time when you have needed and received someone's help and support.
    Explain:
    - the situation you were in and why you needed support
    - how the friend or relation got involved
    - what they did to support you
    - how this support helped you.   (27 marks)

Or

5. **Describe** a person you know well in **two** very different moods.
    Include a description of the following:
    - the person and how you know them so well
    - the two different moods
    - how the person looks and behaves during each mood
    - the causes of the moods and their effects on other people.   (27 marks)